THE COMPLETE LEADER

YOUR PATH TO THE TOP

TRIED AND TRUE PRINCIPLES, GOOD HABITS AND ADVICE TO HELP YOU LEAD

STUDY GUIDE INCLUDED

MARIAN LANGSTON HEARD

AS SEEN WITH BISHOP T.D. JAKES AND PASTOR PAULA WHITE SPEAKING ABOUT LEADERSHIP ON THE 'GOD'S LEADING LADIES' PROGRAM

Table Of Contents

Special thanks to my family

My parents
Ural and Indiana Langston

My husband
Winlow Heard

My sons and daughters-in-law
Gregory and Denielle Pemberton Heard
Derek and Kimberly Main Heard

Sisters
Patricia Bailey Williams
Phyllis Little
Gail Grant

My late brother
Joseph Edmund Langston

Brothers-in-law
Ronald Little, Sr.
Ronald Grant and
The late Leroy Bailey
Sister-in-law
Florence G. Langston

AND

Grandchildren
Michael, Rachael, Preston and Olivia

With deep appreciation
To
Lavette Sealls
Your help made all the difference

This book has been printed as a resource and includes a handy study guide to help you "move to center stage." Each of us plays a role and you need to decide at what point in your life you want to be a supporting player, the co-star or the star, the leader OR sitting on the sidelines and not really participating in all the wonderful challenges and learnings of life and leadership.

This book, in many ways, is quite simple. In fact, some of the chapters will focus on those "simple, basic" things, which can make a world of difference. We must decide how much thought, education, energy and focus we want to put toward the leadership capabilities I believe are in all of us.

God has given us each talents and gifts and we need to listen to His voice to see where in life we will go. We need to remember that there is a gentle hand on our shoulder, a supportive voice in our ear to coach us and boundless love to guide us in our daily decisions.

Who says I am a leader? Who declares you are a leader? What do leaders do? The answers will become clearer as you read the messages and answer the questions as they relate to you and your goals in life.

What do you want to do and when do you want to do it? Whether your goals relate to personal achievements, work-related goals or family dreams, you need to think about leadership in the context of "making things happen." Someone needs to "take the helm," or "give instructions," "lead the way" or "take charge" in any given situation. We all know that children need guidance, so we look to parents and other caring adults to help them. In case of a fire, we all have learned that you shouldn't run, but walk to the nearest exit and in large arenas or sports facilities, there is often an announcement that "in case of an emergency, everyone should wait for instructions." Someone will then take that "lead" and tell us what to do. Will you be giving instructions or always taking instructions? Do you feel comfortable in both these roles? We will explore this information as we move through this book.

Anyone who has ever flown knows the message that is delivered by the pilot or the flight attendant which simply states that "in an emergency, you are asked to follow the instructions and directions of the flight crew."

Loudspeakers everywhere give information and directions. Team captains and managers of every competitive sport from high school, through college and into the ranks of every professional sport; chart the next play, the sequence of behavior and timing on the court or the field.

We see leadership exhibited every day in every walk of life. At a doctor's office, someone has designed the method of greeting, registering and payments. You are instructed what to do when you enter a movie theater. At most religious services, an usher will direct you to your seat or pew and the spiritual leader will guide the service, following his or her printed program giving the sequence of what is going to happen during the service. In each instance, we are following a leader.

Leadership is evident in law enforcement from the officer directing traffic to the first uniformed individual who arrives at the scene of an accident routinely giving us directions.

At our homes, when we are hosting family gatherings, someone has chosen the menu, directed the cooking and serving and others are asked (or as in the case of my family) clearly told where they are needed to make sure that the family dinner is a success.

Leadership. You may not call it that, but that is what has been exhibited. Taking charge and making things happen.

Whether you are running a company and guiding hundreds or thousands of people or whether you are an assistant to a key employee or a novice in a medium or small-sized organization, you need to think about your leadership skills and how you can improve them.

Whether personally or professionally, if you are content where you are and do not want to explore new horizons, there is something to be said about having an appreciation for what you have.

However, if you want to "graduate," and move to a new phase of your life -- then you need to explore your leadership potential and discover some of your latent skills and talents. You might need to push yourself in new areas and expand your thinking. A "new" you will take discipline, energy and determination, however, if you want to have a different role at work, home, church or in the wider community, you might have to make some drastic changes.

Everyone doesn't have great ambition and many are happy just where they are in life. Some others are shy and not confident about their abilities so they have different challenges. If you like who you are and where you are, that's wonderful. Celebrate your contentment.

One of my favorite sayings comes to mind and it's particularly true for those who do not exhibit a grateful heart, can't appreciate what they have and are seemingly never what could be described as "happy." They have been blessed and never acknowledge what God has given them and are constantly complaining and usually appear stressed and driven. Do you have these unhappy people in your life? More later about the time you spend with these "emotional thieves."

The saying is simply, "If you want it all, you will never have enough."

"If you want it all, you will never have enough." Does this saying describe you?

Think about that and find ways to calm down enough to really enjoy yourself, your family, your friends and your work. I speak quite a bit about having the discipline and focus enough to establish these things as a priority both in this book and another recent book called, "TAKE TIME."

"TAKE TIME" contains lots of lists (I am a big list fan) of gentle reminders about having balance, order and purpose in your life.

Now, back to Leadership. Why another book about leadership? Much of the material for this book is taken from sections of hundreds of speeches, commencements, addresses and seminars delivered during the past 40 plus years. In addition, I have added some inspirational phrases (some of my own and others I hope which will give you encouragement and support -- and even a bit of humor).

Recently, as part of the team of "God's Leading Ladies," some of the notes from my presentation called "Lead like a Lady and Win" are also included. The conference called, "God's Leading Ladies" is being led by the very dynamic spiritual leader, Bishop T. D. Jakes of the Potter's House in Dallas, Texas. He and his lovely and talented wife, Serita, organized these sessions to give women a opportunity to learn, grow and celebrate themselves as they learned about relationships, finances, leadership and personal challenges. Thank you both for this incredible opportunity. More about this conference later. The web site is God's Leading Ladies.com.

The book was written to support, encourage, stimulate and challenge you as you strive to be all that God would have you to be. You have skills so I urge you not to waste them. You have strength and I urge you not to waste it. You have dreams and I urge you to take immediate steps to fulfill them!!!

A STUDY GUIDE FORMAT IS INCLUDED - YOU KNOW THE ANSWERS!

In order to encourage you to write your plans, to focus on what you will do and how you will accomplish your goals, we have included space for you to record vital information as a part of your personal planning process. You should note the names of those that have helped you, write about your challenges and how you will overcome each and every obstacle. Push yourself. Applaud yourself. Force yourself to seek help when appropriate and make certain that you have surrounded yourself with those who truly want you to succeed.

Use the Study Guide space to help make your dreams come true.

May you continue to have God's blessings as you continue on your journey.

Marian L. Heard

NOTE:

BIBLE VERSES ARE FROM THE INSPIRATIONAL AND KING JAMES BIBLES.

PREFACE

So much has been written about leadership that I wondered what else could possibly be said and yet, during the past four decades, I have met so many women who are absolutely hungry for advice, counsel and information that I felt that it would be helpful to put these concepts on paper.

Mine is not so much a list of things to do (and yet I believe in making lists and have given you a few to get you started), however, I have also given you a few tips about how to do certain things and options for you to review when you are in certain situations. Also, I talk about some of the pitfalls to avoid in your quest to achieve your own personal and professional goals.

Leadership can be described in many ways and yet we would never get everyone to agree on a single definition of all of the qualities of a leader. Leadership requires certain personality traights, no question, but it also involves intuition and I believe, just common sense. I also believe that a great attitude and lots of energy help as well. Treating people the way you want to be treated, doing what you say you're going to do (and when you promised to do it) as well as looking to the future.

Whatever you are doing now and whatever your dreams, you can certainly increase your odds of getting that promotion, opening that business, moving into a new line of work, negotiating that raise, negotiating that contract, getting your team to move in another direction or organizing the entire institution to support a new strategic plan.

The challenges of leadership are many, however, you have skills, and talents and drive and you will need these and more to fulfill your dreams. Make no mistake; you also need energy, discipline and a will to move forward to win and to achieve. Whether or not you exhibit that will or whether or not people see that quality about you will, in some measure, help you to succeed. People have to believe in you and also believe that you can achieve what you have planned. Yes, everyone likes to be on the winning team, but people also respect effort.

Remember, to have a positive attitude, you should quietly applaud your efforts and your advancement to this point in your life. Also, make a pact with yourself to explore and learn about new things and always, always, remember that in so many instances, it is a combination of the little things that will help you get noticed, get promoted and achieve your goals. Don't eliminate yourself. Don't forget the little things -- they do make a big difference -- and this book is designed to review both the big things and the little things, which I believe, will help you become a better leader.

Let's get started!

I CHRONICLES 28:20 AND DAVID SAID TO SOLOMON HIS SON, BE STRONG AND OF GOOD COURAGE AND DO IT; FEAR NOT, NOR BE DISMAYED: FOR THE LORD GOD EVEN MY GOD WILL BE WITH THEE: HE WILL NOT FAIL THEE, NOR FORSAKE THEE, UNTIL THOU HAST FINISHED ALL THE WORK FOR THE SERVICE OF THE HOUSE OF THE LORD.

PSALM 118:5-6
IN MY ANGUISH I CRIED TO THE LORD, AND HE ANSWERED BY SETTING ME FREE. THE LORD IS WITH ME; I WILL NOT BE AFRAID. WHAT CAN MAN DO TO ME?

HAVE A PLAN AND FOCUS ON THAT PLAN

Whether you're the owner, the CEO, the Executive Vice President, a seasoned Manager or a novice employee, this book contains helpful hints for every stage of management and every stage of leadership. I have provided space for you to add to every list and to insert your own questions and answers. Use this book also as a discussion guide.

If you have finished your career, share your insights with someone else. This book is part textbook and part coaching. Some of the things in this book are things that scores of people have told me that they wished they had known much earlier in their career. There are also some things in this book that will help you no matter where you are on the leadership ladder and, in every instance, you will find yourself challenged and given opportunities to applaud yourself as well as "fill in some blanks." I have found that everyone needs help and I hope that you will find this information helpful to you and to those I hope you will mentor.

What do leaders do? What do leaders need to do? How do you become a leader? When do you know you are a leader?

There are many books, audio tapes and training sessions designed to help leaders, but I believe that in most instances, you have to hone in on the specific areas where you feel you need a boost. The honest among us will quickly tell you their area of greatest challenge. I hope this book will help you and, in turn, you will help others.

We will start with a plan - you determine the timetable - six months, one year, two years, three years or more -- but write it down.

Your success dramatically increases with a written plan. Start to think about the elements of your life (time for self, family, church, work, friends, networking and professional growth as well as community and personal projects). Whatever they are, each component requires a plan because each requires your time, thought, energy and other resources. Review next steps and what should I do first.

Take some quiet thinking time and plan the rest of your life.

12

Notes:

Chapter 1

WHAT DO LEADERS DO?

Leaders plan.

Leaders focus. FOCUS, FOCUS, and FOCUS.

Leaders write down their plans and goals.

You are much more likely to succeed in both your professional life and your personal life if you have a written plan detailing what you plan to do and when you plan to do it. Your plan need not be elaborate, but it should be complete.

Here are the elements of a solid plan:
- Careful homework - make sure that it is documented
- The threats and barriers identified and the specific plan to overcome each one.
- Involvement/communication plan for everyone very early in the process.
- Goal or Vision - What do you want to do? What is the focus of your effort?
- Is your plan easily understood and explained? What will be needed to complete your goal?
- Number of people involved?
- Will they need special training or will you have to hire other talent to complete your goals?
- Timetable?
- Resources needed? Money, equipment, materials? What is your role? The Leader: Other: If you don't have the resources, identify the potential sources and confirm who will be responsible for securing these resources.
- Evaluation - and timing for the evaluation.
- Next steps and timetable for next steps.

This list might be adjusted for specific projects or personal goals such as learning a new skill, losing weight, learning how to swim, understanding how to read financial reports, finishing school or saving to buy a home, however, this would be a pretty good list to start with as you review your own plans both as a leader and as an individual.

I'm a big dreamer. I like big ideas and sweeping goals. So sweeping that I like to create some excitement and people can see that, with their effort and participation, we will accomplish something really wonderful, something really significant. I'm going to encourage you to think BIG and be a dreamer! It doesn't cost anything to dream, so dream BIG!!!

Are you taking a risk? Absolutely! Should you lower your expectations and not have a bold plan? No! Timidity will be noted and you will have a much harder time in the future if you are not confident enough to present a big idea, but instead your plan is not exciting or even interesting and is merely called the "same old plan" with a new name. This is not good. Most people like big ideas and would rather put their energies into something that is truly going to make a difference either in the company, the community and/or the lives of thousands of people.

You can also create excitement with smaller efforts, but you have to use great skills in making smaller projects, little ideas, generate that kind of commitment.

Review the elements again and again and then act. It doesn't matter that you have great ideas if they remain in your head. It doesn't matter that you have fantastic plans to share if they remain just plans. You have to move. You have to act. You have to make a decision. You have to work to make your dreams a reality. You have to be enthusiastic and formulate a plan to sell your idea.

If your idea cannot be completed without the support of your entire organization, or in my instance, often an entire city or region, then you have to also plan the best way to introduce your plan and get people on board with a "shared vision." If tens or hundreds or thousands of people are being asked to help fulfill your dream or complete your goal or the goal for the entire community, you must -- early in the process -- have acceptance and the ability to generate a feeling that this is everyone's goal and not just your goal. People will want to share in the planning, the review, and the confirmation of the key elements and, of course, in the completion.

Most people like to be with a winner, so you have to make sure that from the start, you have generated enthusiasm, exhibited the will to succeed and have built up enough credibility so that people will believe that you can indeed be successful.

Having the credibility of past success is a powerful tool, however, everyone has a first idea or a first project and you just have to work harder to get people on your team and make sure that you exhibit enough confidence so that they know you are determined to lead them to the victory.

In my work at the United Way, we have had a lot of experience getting people to work with us during the early "idea" phase of many efforts, to help us to confirm a goal and a strategy, suggest adjustments for the timetable and "sign up" to be a key part of the effort to help children in a special way, under the aegis of a project called, "Success By Six." Started in Minneapolis, this program has a simple goal. The goal is simply making sure that children are ready to learn and progress by the time they are six years of age. There is an early intervention strategy in place as well, so that programs focus on what happens as soon as that child is born. This wonderful effort won the national Mary Gates Award for Community Partnerships. This Award is named for the late mother of Bill Gates (the Microsoft co-founder) and is a major accomplishment in the national United Way movement.

We needed hundreds of people to help us with our legislative efforts to get access to health care for 163,000 uninsured children in Massachusetts. This was a BIG idea -- a very BIG idea. We worked with a broad-based group of representatives from the community and after this effort was successful, it was easier to get regional and statewide participation for an after-school effort and an initiative called, "Keeping Kids on Track. This initiative is also viewed as extremely successful and has the very important components of tutoring, mentoring and safe after-school support which is so desperately needed for working parents. KKOT as we call it just won a major partnership award from the National Broadcasters Association for its broadcast partner, WCVB-TV, Channel 5 (the ABC affiliate in Boston), Keyspan Energy and our United Way.

Review your goals?

Are you focused? Are your goals clear? Can they be easily explained?

What do you want to accomplish?

Can others articulate this goal and know what you want to accomplish?

How will you get momentum?

How will you keep people engaged in the project and make certain they are on board during the entire project?

What could cause you to fail?

Do you have the right people? Are they appropriately trained?

When do you want to finish?

What will change when you are successful?

Can everyone agree on what will change? Do they understand the value of their involvement?

How will you define success?

Make certain that you have reviewed all of the elements of good planning, confirmed all the data and have enough involvement so that you have the appropriate help you need to get to the goal line.

You will be the cheerleader, so make sure that you have clear goals and that everyone involved can explain what you want just as clearly as you can. If not, you have a communications challenge on your hands or you might not have complete acceptance of your plan. The acceptance is extremely important, since you don't want to confirm a 60 day timetable and then find out that no one on your team really liked the idea in the first place and didn't really give the project or plan the appropriate attention and focus and, in fact, if this is the case, you will have significant challenges trying to keep your project on target.

It is important to have a quick start -- gain some traction, some momentum and let everyone know that you are moving ahead. Let them know that their efforts and their participation has been critical to the early victory and they will be encouraged to remain focused and energized. Make sure that any early success is quickly and thoroughly communicated to everyone involved.

These progress reports will encourage your team members and their positive feedback will also encourage you.

Has everyone involved confirmed that they agree with the plan?

Have you confirmed who is responsible for every element and their individual timetable for completion of their phase of the effort?

Are you ready for the challenge?

Do you have the will to win? Do you have the focus? The stamina? The determination?

What else do you need to do to get ready to win and succeed?

Joshua 1:9 Have not I commanded thee? Be strong and of a good courage; be not afraid, neither be thou dismayed: for the Lord thy God is with thee whithersoever thou goest.

> "Leadership is action, not position"
> Donald H. McGannon

> "If you find a path with no obstacles, it probably doesn't lead anywhere."
> Frank A. Clark

> "What would we be if we had no courage to attempt any thing?"
> Vincent Van Gogh

> "You can fail so very often, but you are not a failure until you give up."
> Source unknown

Remember, when you are thinking about the time needed to complete careful homework, make certain that you have thoroughly reviewed all of your options and calmly reviewed your options -- that if you don't find time to do it right the first time -- when are you going to find time to do it over?

Chapter 2

GIVE YOUR BEST EFFORT

Make sure that you have completed careful homework, not just for special projects, but every single day. This is important for you as an individual and as a leader. It is critical that you have researched the data and, in some instances, this might require some extra time searching the web or visiting the library. When you are working on a critical project, make certain that you complete this research yourself or that you have delegated it to someone who has proved that he or she will make certain that the information is correct.

Don't forget, when you give the report or sign your name, you own the information, so it is imperative that you take the time to read the information and look for glaring errors as well as review the information with the person who has conducted the research.

There are few things worse than stating a fact or an opinion based on facts you have been given by someone else only to find out that you do not have the current or the correct information. Don't let this happen to you. Make certain that when you sign your name and "own" the information, that you are certain that it is current and correct.

In mid-2003, there were daily reports that the State of the Union Address given early in 2003 by the President contained false information. With Congressional hearings, reports from London, conflicting reports from the CIA and the White House, we have a glaring example of what faulty research looks like. We also have a great example of what "accepting responsibility looks like." The President declared that, "it was my error." Life's lessons and leadership examples every day -- watch and learn!!!

Recent corporate bankruptcies tell us that inaccurate and doctored reports, "creative" accounting records and conflicting e-mails remind us about careful documentation and the need to verify information before we sign our name and make public declarations. The results of inaccurate information can often de-rail careers and lead to financial ruin.

Your reputation will be based on the work you perform.

Have you read about the subject?

Have you confirmed your facts?

Are you clear about the history, the current situation and have you reviewed the elements which might impact the future use of your data?

Have you studied all the options?

Be known for careful homework.

Guard your reputation.

Many people think that shortcuts are the way of life. Do not get into the habit of taking shortcuts. If you are currently cutting corners to get work completed, you should evaluate whether your work load is appropriate (many people have increased work responsibilities because of layoffs in their company), however, your work load should be challenging, but not so onerous that you are never able to get caught up or indeed, never get ahead. You should carefully evaluate this if you are taking shortcuts to keep up and also if you are working longer hours.

The situation might call for a meeting with your supervisor -- or if you are the owner -- the President -- the Chief Executive Officer -- you might need additional employees to help with the increased business and responsibilities.

Women sometimes have a harder time than men gaining credibility and often have not had as many experiences either presenting the information or being in enough meetings to watch and learn. Granted, much improvement has occurred and women are in virtually every line of work and hold many titles -- some of these titles would have been impossible two or three decades ago. Nonetheless, many women tell me that they feel like they are ignored, their suggestions and ideas dismissed and they are not always given as much credit as their male counterparts.

We still read that salaries are a continuing issue and women lag men; and women and men of color lag white males in far too many categories. We know that women have achieved in many challenging fields and things are changing every year, however, once an opportunity has been given, women often feel added pressure because "they are the first" in a particular position or they do not have a male or female mentor to help them navigate the organization.

Women need to be careful that in their quest to be accepted, that they are not putting themselves in situations where they will tarnish their reputations.

Legends of women, we know, can more than hold their own in any situation. In fact, we all know of instances where women have indeed done a much better job than a man they replaced. However, our challenge is often getting more women to a level where they have the opportunity to make meaningful contributions and be in the real "decision-making" meetings and be clearly identified in the organization as a part of "senior management" or the "management committee" or "chairman's committee" or whatever the key group is called.

I encourage women to use the time before meetings, during meals and other less formal opportunities at the workplace to strengthen relationships, particularly with those you work with on an infrequent basis and those you would like to know better. Remember, if you want to move up with an organization, you must make sure that your decisions about where you meet and with whom are indeed appropriate.

Today's working environments are often challenging. Women are being asked to travel alone or with groups of men and find themselves away from their spouses and families on frequent occasions. Women must make sure that they plan ahead and think through what they will do while on the road. Make careful decisions about where to eat and with whom and to remember that there is really an invisible line regarding behavior with other employees, peers and particularly with subordinates.

Are you asked to travel for your organization or company?

Do you know what you will do if you are asked to travel alone? With a group?

Have you planned your evening meals and other activities?

How will you keep in touch with your family?

Have you tracked your hours at the office, on the road and then getting caught up on your deskwork?

You might not be able to do much about the schedule, but when special family occasions pose a conflict, you must learn to say, "I have a commitment and will not be able to travel." If you work for a "family-friendly" company, surely your previous willingness to travel will afford you some credit, however, if you are constantly challenged about the time you want to spend with your family and if your travel often involves weekend trips, you might need to review your position as well as your future with the company.

Have you had to cancel family plans for work-related travel?

What are your plans should this be a constant request?

My suggestion is to have a private and honest conversation about your travel/conflicting meeting schedule so that your employer is aware of your issues. Make sure that you have careful records and indicate that you are only interested in doing a great job (not just good), however, your work/travel hours are causing major conflicts and you would like to review the schedule and work to negotiate something that is acceptable to you and your supervisor.

If you are the owner or the CEO, I hope that you are doing all you can to make certain that your employees have balance in their world. They will be happier and more productive knowing that their superior cares for them as a human being.

For those scheduling meetings -- and this is important -- watch the calendar and be sensitive about major holidays, the start of school in August or September and school vacation weeks. There isn't a working mother (or father) anywhere in America who doesn't fret about making certain that he/she can be at home for some extra time during these important days in the life of her child and also have some flexibility in making sure to spend some quality family time during holiday periods.

Ruth 3:ll And now, my daughter, fear not; I will do thee all that thou request; for all the city of my people doth know that thou art a virtuous woman.

Proverbs 12:4 A virtuous woman is a crown to her husband: but she that maketh ashamed is as rottenness in his bones.

Proverbs 31:10 Who can find a virtuous woman? For her price is far above rubies.

Proverbs19: 20-21 Listen to advice and accept instruction, and in the end you will be wise. Many are the plans in a man's heart, but it is the Lord's purpose that prevails.

> "Vision without action is merely a dream. Action without vision just passes time. Vision with action can change the world. A true leader must first see an idea as opportunity, then choose to act upon it."
>
> Joel Barker

> "God wants to use you - stumbling and all - but he won't do so if you refuse to get up."
>
> Charles R. Swindoll

As youngsters, we all remember the saying about happiness. If you wanted happiness for a short time, you should take a nap, but if you wanted happiness for a lifetime, then you should help someone else.

VOLUNTEERING

Whether it is at church, in your community groups or for a professional organization, find time to volunteer. Make time to help others and you will be amazed at how this will enrich your life. Your problems will not loom quite as large when you visit a hospital and read to the elderly who are not only frail, but lonely as well. Your care and attention will truly benefit two people -- the person you help -- and you in the most profound ways. To volunteer, simply call your local United Way office and they will help you find a place, a time and a way for you to make this very personal connection with others.

Chapter 3

INTERVIEWING - (GREAT REMINDERS WHETHER YOU ARE HIRING OR SEEKING A POSITION)

Know the law.

It's a simple statement, however, make sure that you have taken time to review the current laws regarding interviewing. There are certain personal questions regarding age and other issues that are illegal. You should know what they are so that you are prepared when you are getting ready to hire someone or if you are looking for work.

If you don't have a labor lawyer in the family or your company does not have one, then you should review the following:

> If you are working for a company and the employee has been hired through a central personnel system and then assigned to your department, then someone else has been responsible for the primary interviewing. If you, on the other hand, must interview prospective candidates, you would be wise to review the laws with your human resource officials.

> If you are the CEO/Director or own your own company, you might want to get a briefing either through professional human resource organizations or by contacting the local Bar Association to determine if they have workshops/seminars you can attend. Also, check the courses at your community colleges.

> If you are going to be interviewed for a job, it will be very helpful if you have read all you can about the company. Try to talk to current and former employees about the work environment and, again, know your rights and which questions are permissible and which are not.

Some basic reminders about interviewing if you are seeking a job:

Have you obtained current information about the company and read it?

Have you conducted further research to make certain you have a clear understanding about the company or organization?

Do you have a clear understanding about the position you are seeking?

Do you feel that you are qualified and can you clearly articulate why you are qualified?

Can you quickly and calmly state why you would be an asset to the company? (Write these statements and practice them until they are clear and you can state them concisely.)

Do you know others who work there?

Are you clear about your expected salary?

Are you prepared to negotiate? If so, are you clear about the specifics of what you need and want? Do you have a list of your most important items or issues?

Do you believe that you will have opportunities to get promotions, have a long-term career and be in an environment where you will learn and grow?

Have you asked about training opportunities?

Have you practiced your handshake (not too firm)?

Have you conducted mock interviews with someone who will give you honest feedback?

A workd about references. Please ask permission before giving someone's name as a reference for you. Call and alert them about your job search and share as many details as possible so that they can stress your "great qualities" and particularly the ones you want them to emphasize.

FOCUS, FOCUS, FOCUS.

Always check the clothes you are going to wear. Check the buttons, the hems, the linings and the collars and cuffs. Make certain that the clothes are not soiled and are cleaned and pressed. After all, you only have this first interview to make that great impression. Often, people are called back for additional interviews with their potential supervisors or others in the company they will be working with, however, if you don't make that great impression during the first interview, it is highly unlikely you will ever know about those other people or other great opportunities, because you won't have that second chance.

Don't eliminate yourself.

Make certain that you have checked your shoes. They should be polished and appropriate for the job you want. Drive by the company early in the morning or in the afternoon and watch what people who work there are wearing. Also, you can ask someone who currently works at the company - or the person conducting your interview - if the company has a dress code or a policy about the dress required for certain positions or on certain days. Many companies have vacillated between business casual, business attire at all times or casual on Fridays. Some companies have a policy of causal from the 4th of July until Labor Day. You are always safe wearing conservative clothes and, unless you confirm otherwise, going to an interview wearing business clothes. That is, of course, suit and tie for men and an appropriate suit or tailored dress for women.

Speaking about suits for women, I recommend that women get out three suits from their closet.

Try on the first suit. Sit in front of a full-length mirror and check the length of the skirt. Make sure that the skirt isn't too short. If you live in North Carolina and you can see all the way to Chicago, take off that skirt and think twice about ever wearing it again. It is obviously too short.

Next try on the second suit. If the blouse has buttons and the buttons are supposed to go north and south -- up and down -- and they are pulling east and west, then that blouse is obviously too small, so take if off.

Try on the third suit and, just like the children's story of Goldilocks, hopefully, it is "just right." If not, you will need to go shopping.

A little humor, but all too often, women rush to the meeting or the interview without first checking the view from all angles in a full-length mirror. I know that you have seen both of the above "suits" and wondered if the person owned a mirror.

Just a reminder -- get a full-length mirror.

For men and women, check your hair and hands. Make sure that your hair has been neatly combed and that your nails are clean and well shaped. These are simple things and you might flip through this section, however, the careers of many people have stopped before they got started because they have not practiced the basics regarding appearance and interviewing.

If you like wearing nail polish, stick to a muted tone. Avoid very bright reds and decorated false nails. Some women have two or three colors on their nails and often they have different designs. Please save those for your personal time or weekend activities. These designs are not appropriate for most work settings and you might not be lucky enough to have someone quietly tell you that. It is one of the little things that might eliminate you. Remember, don't eliminate yourself.

For men, watch the suits as well. Make sure that your suit is appropriate for the season and fits well.

Ladies, if you can hear your jewelry, it is too busy. No dangling bracelets or multiple layers of jewelry. Also, if you have pierced a body part other than your ears, please remove the jewelry or stones before seeking a job.

Remember that the interview is likely to take place behind closed doors, so not spraying on too much perfume or cologne would be appreciated. You don't know if the person conducting the interview is allergic to perfume or if the one you have chosen will be overpowering in a small room with the door closed.

Don't eliminate yourself. Check the little things.

A reminder - don't forget to brush your teeth. Also, keep dental floss and mouthwash handy, particularly if the interview is over a meal or after a meal. Don't wait until you get in the car after your interview or have arrived home before discovering that a piece of lettuce is stuck in between your two front teeth. No garlic or onions please and, if you are being interviewed over a meal, no pasta with tomato sauce. Don't order anything that could spill or stain your clothes. Safe bets: a tuna salad, plain penne pasta with white sauce on the side (easy to add a few spoons on the pasta and not worry about the sauce dripping on your shirt or suit.)

Remember to watch your table manners if you are having a meal-related interview. No licking. No licking. It is not only unsightly, but unsanitary as well. We've all seen children licking their fingers and we quickly intervene and remind them that they have been playing on the floor or outside in the mud and that their hands are dirty. So it goes with adults. They might not have been playing on the floor or in the mud, but they have been shaking hands, opening doors, and handling the mail and other papers. No licking, no licking, no licking!!!

You might have picked up the habit of licking your fingers as a child -- before you learned how to use a napkin -- and now (as I have observed many people) -- start at the thumb and lick every finger on both hands. It may be common at your home, but for those who want to move up in the business world, again a reminder, no licking. Don't eliminate yourself. Watch your table manners!

The recent viral (and Norwalk) outbreaks on cruise ships and in China, Canada and other parts of the world are reminders about the need to constantly wash our hands. So, if adults have been shaking hands and handling doors and then picking up buffet or other commonly used utensils as well as handling menus and other table items, you have to wonder if their hands are clean as they reach to shake your hand and then proceed to lick their own hands.

Don't eliminate yourself.

If you have carefully prepared and added these tips to the ones that you already know, don't be too disappointed if you don't get hired for that particular position. Try and try again. Always give yourself great points for being able to have a great interview. You will feel much more confident and comfortable if you have done all you possibly can to make a great impression, spoken with clarity about what value you would bring to the organization and have explained some of the things you have already accomplished. Just remember to practice and be a great listener to every question posed in your interview.

If possible, when you are not selected, call and try to determine why you weren't selected and get feedback from the person who conducted the interview. This information will be invaluable during future interviews.

Leaders are mindful of the big picture, but they also watch the little details.

One earring per ear is really quite sufficient, unless this is an interview for a rock band. If you are interviewing for a position in an executive's office or in a place where you will be greeting the public, be warned.

I have noticed that some women are wearing multiple earrings (not just two, but three or more) and, unless this is the norm for the company you wish to work for, it is not something that will guarantee that you will be asked back for the next interview. Watch those exiting from the company and, again, see what the dress code is for those who currently work there. Don't eliminate yourself. Don't forget the little things.

Ladies, if offered water, please ask for a glass, if you see one handy. If not, pass. Try to avoid drinking water from the bottle. Yes, please don't!

I know, I know, I know -- you might say, "you see everyone drinking out of bottles," however, I am going to suggest that you try to use a glass or a straw. You are a lot less likely to spill water on yourself waiting for your interview and glasses and straws usually don't require that you have a napkin to check whether or not you have a few extra drops of water on your upper lip or your face. Also, drinking from the bottle often causes choking and this is not the way to get attention.

Clean your glasses. The spots you see from the inside can also be seen from the outside. This is something I have to remind myself about and when I do clean my glasses, I am amazed at the number of very large spots that I know must have appeared to look very messy. Don't forget the little things.

This is a very important reminder. Make certain that the brief case or purse you have has been organized so that you can quickly retrieve anything you need for the interview. It will be very disconcerting if you have to "dig around" to find a pen or an extra copy of your resume. Take time to get organized. Don't eliminate yourself. It's the little things.

Remember to try to relax. You know what your strengths are and you have an answer ready about what you are doing to work on your challenges. You have prepared yourself. You are ready for the next step. You can articulate what you can add to the organization. You have read all you can and are able to discuss the new products, the new acquisition, the price of the stock, the news of the day, the issues in the community, the role you hope to play and will be able to handle the tough questions, because you have practiced, practiced and practiced again. Use a mirror if you need one and get a trusted friend or advisor to help you. Work on the key things and you will feel an air of confidence and it will show.

Always call and re-confirm your appointment. Even though most people have voice mail and other means of contact, sometimes technology fails us, so you should always re-confirm the time, place, office location and name of the person you are going to see. Have this information handy when you are checking into the building.

In most large cities, the security in place now requires a photo identification as well as confirmation that your name is indeed on the list of expected visitors.

Remember that this process might take up to 20 minutes, so leave yourself extra time so that you are not late.

It is very important that you are not late for the interview, however, arriving early will also give you a chance to relax for a few minutes, collect your thoughts and get on "your game face." Finding a job, doing well in an interview and imparting the most important facts about yourself all require focus. Focus, Focus, Focus. You don't want to be rushed or late for this very important meeting.

Always, always, always write a thank you letter to the person who has conducted the interview. Please write this note immediately; again expressing your desire to join the company. Check your grammar and your spelling and verify the spelling and title of the person you are writing. I often receive letters with both my name and title spelled incorrectly and sometimes sent to the wrong address. I know right away that the person has not done careful homework.

Don't eliminate yourself.

Do you know as many details as possible to help you "win" in the job interview?

Have you had enough practice to answer anticipated questions?

Have you been honest on your resume? Is your resume up to date?

Have you clearly identified your accomplishments?

Muriel Siebert, the first woman seated for the New York Stock Exchange indicated that her first resume stated that she had not graduated from college. So, after being rebuffed during her first interview because of that fact, she misrepresented her past on her resume.

She was lucky and had a chance to correct the information several years later, however, she was by that time very successful. You might not be so lucky, so make sure that your resume contains just the facts. You would not want to miss out on a great job, a wonderful opportunity or a great promotion because you misrepresented yourself on your resume.

Most companies and organizations have very strict policies in place, which call for severe sanctions (including immediate dismissal) if it is determined, that your resume contains false information.

Is your resume accurate?

Are the details about your education correct?

Is your resume free from misspelled words?

Does your cover letter have correct grammar?

Have you asked someone who is concerned about your success to review both your resume and your letters?

Have you considered getting professional help from a resume service to help tell your story in a more powerful way, using words and phrases to more quickly capture attention and possibly give you an edge?

Do you have different resumes so that your focus is pertinent to a particular position?

Do you feel that you will do a great job? (Notice I didn't say good job.)

Yes, confidence is important. Don't forget the little things.

I Samuel 2:4
The bows of the mighty men are broken, and they that stumbled are girded with strength.

Isaiah 40: 31
But those who wait on the Lord shall renew their strength, they shall mount up with wings like eagles, they shall run and not be

weary, they shall walk, and not faint.

Matthew 11: 30
For my yoke is easy and my burden is light.
I Thessalonians 2: 8
But as we have been approved by God to be entrusted with the gospel even so we speak, not as pleasing men, but God who tests our hearts.

"The shame is not in failing, the shame is in not trying."`
From my parents - Ural and Indiana Langston

FIRING EMPLOYEES

A word about firing employees.

Again, know the law.

Also, long before you have reached the decision about firing someone, be sure you have carefully checked the files and the documentation is clear. Make certain that the employee has been carefully warned, given the opportunity to improve, given a written statement about the issues and signed the warning notices as well as the personal action plan for improvement.

If you have carefully documented the issues -- and I do mean carefully -- then the person you are firing really should not be surprised!

Get ready!!!

Firing an employee is serious business. After all, he or she has hopes and dreams, obligations and usually an expectation of continued employment, so it is critical that you are prepared. Know the law and I recommend that you have a witness so that you are protected and your organization has an objective third party to document the meeting as well.

Many people who are fired react emotionally and will sometimes make threats against you personally or against the company, that is why a witness is so important.

If you have ever been fired from a job, you might or might not have had a good experience. What you ask, could possibly be a good experience in getting fired? As I stated above, most people really aren't surprised and when they are over the initial embarrassment, they will recall the earlier meetings, plans for improvement and warnings -- both verbal and written -- that they chose to ignore or perhaps they just weren't capable of doing the job.

I believe that it is a rare instance when other employees don't know when someone is not carrying his or her weight, so your action (if you don't wait too long) will usually be applauded. The other employees don't want to feel like someone else is "getting away with something" and you, as the leader have shown favoritism or turned a blind eye to the problem.

If you have any, and I do mean any, questions about the law, remember to consult with the persons responsible for personnel matters in your organization or, of necessary, an attorney specializing in employment and labor law.

Try to make the firing as humane as possible. Remember that you would want to have someone treat you with dignity if the situations were reversed.

If necessary, practice, practice, practice.

Remember to document, document, and document. Also, when it is a critical meeting, have a witness.

Have you reviewed the files?

Would you say that your written policies and procedures about appropriate notification and whether other remedies have been tried?

Are you clear about the employee's rights?

Have you checked to see what benefits are due the employee? (If you have a special person or department for human resource issues, someone else might take care of this or you might need to review these matters ahead of time.)

Have you made sure that the timing of the firing is appropriate?

Have you confirmed when that person will leave the building and have you made certain that he or she doesn't have access to the computers or other company property?

Who will be with the employee as he or she gathers personal property?

Make certain that you have not eliminated yourself and, if you have been given either verbal or written warnings, review all of the personnel policies and schedule appropriate meetings with your supervisor to review what steps you need to take to get "back on track."

Know the law. The time you spend learning new things is never wasted.

I Timothy 5:17
Pray without ceasing.

Proverbs 15:1-2 A gentle answer turns away wrath, but a harsh word stirs up anger. The tongue of the wise commends knowledge, but the mouth of the fool gushes folly.

"On every level of life, from housework to the heights of

power, in all judgement and all efforts to get things done, hurry and impatience are the sure marks of an amateur."
Evelyn Underhill

"One of the greatest pieces of economic wisdom is to know what you do not know."
John Kenneth Galbrath

Ask for God's guidance as you review critical employment issues. Get support from those who have your best interests at heart.

Notes:_____

_____

_____

_____

_____

_____

_____

_____

_____

_____

_____

_____

_____

_____

_____

_____

_____

Chapter 4

KNOW HOW YOUR ORGANIZATION FUNCTIONS

Make certain that you have kept up to date regarding your company. It is often a challenge, particularly if your company is growing rapidly, you don't work at the headquarters facility or if the company's turnover is such that you are constantly working with new people. This aspect of leadership will often require discipline. Discipline to read any new information, discipline to make certain that you understand new products, information about your organization that has appeared in the newspaper or information that has been distributed within your company. Don't just file the information, read it and, when necessary, find an opportunity to discuss the details so that you are prepared to participate in the conversation when these items are discussed. Discipline yourself to keep up to date.

INCLUSIVENESS/DIVERSITY/VALUING DIVERSITY

The phrase "value diversity" is used quite extensively, and rightly so. I believe that we will only get it right when we acknowledge that we can "learn something from people who are different." In other words, no matter what a person's background, skin color or the religious preference, we all need to remind ourselves that, "I might be better tomorrow than I am today, because that different person taught me a skill or I learned something about the way they live." That, my friends, does have real value and gives us an appreciation of all of God's creations.

Does your organization have a written statement about inclusiveness? Have you reviewed it?

It is also important to realize that all types of people buy products and, no matter what your business sells or what products it makes, people who look differently are probably going to buy them or use your services. Be prepared for different names, different cultures, the celebration of different holidays and often preferences for different food.

Be gracious and open and know that a welcoming posture will be noted. Leaders understand that they set the example in their organization. Whatever the behavior is, it will be the model. Make certain that you understand that you are being watched and your behavior will be viewed as the accepted and acceptable behavior.

Set the tone and remember that you are the example for others.

THANK YOU, THANK YOU VERY MUCH.

Find frequent opportunities to thank people. Let employees know that you appreciate their effort, their loyalty and their support. The "thank you" does not have to be elaborate, but it should be SINCERE and when appropriate, done publicly within the company and announced so that all who can will be aware that you have cited great performance, terrific customer service, the completion of a task or for service when employees have completed 1, 5, 10 or a greater number of years.

SHARE THE CREDIT

Whatever is going on in your company, when progress is confirmed, find a way to applaud others. Never, never take all of the credit and make certain to cite those responsible for either the progress or the successful completion of projects or major goals.

Saying "thank you" is a big part of who I am and I want to encourage you to emphasize this aspect of your life as well. How many times have you thought about a person and realize that he or she never, never says thank you. No matter how much effort you have put into a task, no matter how much you have adjusted your schedule -- it doesn't seem to matter and has not produced a simple acknowledgement. Don't you forget to say those magic words. They mean a great deal to most people!

Make certain that you have not forgotten someone. Make a list of the names or have someone verify all the names, particularly if you are going to make a public statement.

BE READY, BE READY, BE READY

Even small organizations are increasingly complex and dynamic. What worked yesterday might not be appropriate today, so you have to be flexible and ready to respond to different issues. Be ready. Keep up to date about new business procedures, technological changes and policy and procedural techniques. If you don't know, ask. Make sure that you ask before you respond so that your information is as current as possible.

DEVELOP YOUR OWN STYLE OF MANAGEMENT

What is your style? Are you approachable?

What kind of leader are you?

Are you open and accessible?

What will you do to change your style if you believe that the one you have adopted is not really getting you the results you want? You have to ask yourself, "is this working?"

You might not even have a name for your style. Maybe you haven't

even thought about it, however, you should. Know who you are --
see yourself as others see you!

Do you know what's going on in your company or organization.

Are you able to keep up to date about the critical components of
your business?

As you always the last one to know key things?

Are projects being started without your involvement?

Make sure you understand your strengths. Make certain that you
have continued to build on your strengths and that you are, in fact,
well known for at least one of your fine qualities.

"Play to your strengths."   This is a favorite saying of mine,
however, we all know that each of us has different skills. Use all
the skills God gave you. Work on improving them and also work
on those areas where you are not as strong.

A healthy exercise is to review how you have handled problems.
None of us is perfect, so we are bound to make mistakes, however,
reviewing how you might now handle that same situation if you had
incorporated some of the new things you have learned, is key.

Different experiences will give us different perspectives; so that our
approach to problems will reflect the new things we have learned
and, hopefully, prevent us from making the same mistakes again.

A great question to ask if you are interviewing someone is "how have you handled your past mistakes?" If you are going to be interviewed, you should have a response ready in case the person who will be interviewing you poses this question.

If you need a certain skill in your work area, make certain that you look for that skill when you are hiring. Don't be afraid. Skilled people want to work with other talented people. You can learn from someone who is a good match and a great compliment for your skills. You can help each other improve.

Some people really fear having someone around who might appear to be smarter or have a specialty they do not possess. Try to think about this in a different way. Try to learn from everyone, particularly when another person has a skill that you want to strengthen. Learn, learn, and learn.

MANAGEMENT STYLE

Earlier I asked if you knew your management style. I have identified mine and it is modeled after a movie title.

"The Good, the Bad and the Ugly," is a famous so-called spaghetti western, so named because some were made in Italy and were also produced with modest budgets. The name of this movie fits my form of management.

I want to know "The Good, the Bad and the Ugly" - I want to know it now - and not necessarily in that order!

Everyone who works for me knows this about me. I don't want to be blindsided or have critical information that someone knows and I have not had the opportunity to know so that I can factor it into my decision-making process. I don't know a CEO or anyone in any position of authority (not a parent or a grandparent or a supervisor at any level) who wants to be blindsided.

How often have you had to ask at home or at work, "Why didn't you tell me about that?" You will need to make sure that you have an approachable posture and that people are not afraid to give you bad news at home or at work.

Information is critical and you must exhibit a willingness to listen and, at times, hear the bad news and I do mean the really bad news. If you let people know that you are that kind of manager, director or leader then they will feel empowered to help you succeed.

Think about your teen-age years. Were your parents or those who raised you open to hearing the bad news? Is your spouse open to hearing bad news? Are you open to hearing the ugly facts?

INFORMATION NOW
Everyone knows I want all the pertinent information. Tell me the facts. We all need to know the facts. You can't make good decisions if you don't have all the information. Some CEO's have often punished or maligned the messenger, so many employees are often afraid to deliver bad news.

No, you can't know everything, however, the chain of command or the organizational structure should be such that you are aware of the most important issues within your organization. If not, you need to find out why.

So it is in family situations. Someone who has damaged the car is often afraid to break the bad news. Would you want a family member to tell you that he or she had an accident and the car was badly damaged or would you want the first call to be from the insurance company? You lost an important item belonging to someone else and are wondering how to approach the owner. You promised to do something by a certain date and now find that you have to change your plans. Well, we have all lived through these and many more situations and yet, in the workplace, fear often surfaces when you have to be the one to bring the bad news, particularly if you know it will not be well received. You need only remember -- when bad news has to be delivered -- the motto is the sooner, the better!!!

Remember, if you are the one receiving the report, make sure that you never, never "blame the messenger." Your major complaints might be that the information is not timely or that it is not complete. You will need to make sure that the information is clear and complete. If there is a serious problem, make certain to get as much information as quickly as possible. Only then can you decide what to do.

I'm going to say it again; you never want to make people afraid to tell you bad news. Remember that you need to have an approachable posture. Employees at most levels need to feel that, if not a direct line, a formal documented structure is in place to get information of a critical nature to you, if, indeed you are the leader.

Some large organizations have hot lines, others have ombudpersons. The rules regarding the responsibilities for the ombudsperson will be different at different companies, however, their role is generally to listen to complaints, review issues and speak on behalf of the employee. Still, other companies have centered this function in the Personnel or Human Resources Departments. In smaller companies the chain of command is usually a lot less formal, so you should make sure that you know what the policies and procedures are in your company and whether you are the leader, the supervisor or an associate, you know the procedures and/or the rules.

What if you suspect that someone is breaking the law? Your personnel policies should provide clear guidance about how to proceed. If not, find out who in your company or organization is the most appropriate person who might give you guidance. In any instance, it is always helpful if you have documented your complaint or issue or if you are not clear about a potential problem, you have the specifics about your issue very clearly outlined so that you can either share the appropriate information or you can determine next steps.

If you responsible for establishing the policy about reporting illegal or unethical behavior, you will need to make certain that everyone has a copy of any such policy and, if necessary, you should schedule a meeting or a series of meetings to review the policy.

As an example, we had mandatory meetings at the United Way to review the law regarding sexual harassment. In this way, our organization was doing all it could to make certain that every employee knew the law and hence, if there happened to be a problem, we had made an honest effort to alert everyone that inappropriate behavior would not be tolerated and reviewed the laws regarding consequences for employees and for our United Way. Again, know the law or get help with key issues so that you are getting current information.

Once you have received information about a critical issue or a crisis, you might need to make certain that the information has been verified and then decide who within the organization needs to know. You would then make a decision and, if needed, announce the decision to those who need to know. Remember, if you are the supervisor or the owner, review with the appropriate employees so that this key information is relayed in a timely manner.

Do you have someone who will keep you informed?

Have you not known about key events?

Have you been blindsided? If so, what were the circumstances?

What are you going to do to prevent this from happening in the future?

Do you present an open, approachable posture?

Do you strive for excellence and precision -- not perfection?

Do you give yourself credit for making progress?

How did you react the last time someone told you some very bad news?

How would you change your reaction in the future?

Ken Blanchard, one of the country's great business minds and one of the authors of "The One Minute Manager" which was an extraordinary success was one of my instructors at the University of Massachusetts at Amherst. Ken is also the co-author of several other books including the wonderful, "The Servant Leader" written with Phil Hodges.

He believes that there are four basic leadership styles: Directing, Coaching, Supporting and Delegating. Understanding your leadership style will not only help you do a better job, but will give you a great blueprint for the areas you will need to strengthen. Confirming your basic leadership approach will also help as you hire, particularly if you want to compliment your style and select someone who will help to add depth to your company.

It would be helpful for you to spend some time reading about leadership and leadership styles and for you to review the elements of yours on a regular basis. This is a very helpful exercise.

Daniel 1:17 As for these four children, God gave them knowledge and skill in all learning and wisdom and Daniel had understanding in all visions and dreams.

Acts 2:17 And it shall come to pass in the last days, saith God, I will pour out of my Spirit upon all flesh; and your sons and your daughters shall prophesy, and your young men shall dream dreams.

1 Chronicles 22:13 Then shalt thou prosper, if thou takest heed to fulfill the statutes and judgments, which the Lord charged Moses with concerning Israel: be strong, and of good courage, dread not, nor be dismayed.

"We grow greatly by dreams. All big men are dreamers. They see things in the soft haze of a spring day or in the red fire of a long winter's evening. Some of us let these great dreams die, but others nourish, protect and nurse them through bad days 'til they bring them to the sunshine and light which comes always to those who sincerely hope that their dreams will come true."
Woodrow T. Wilson

"People think that at the top there isn't much room. They tend to think of it as an Everest. My message is that there is tons of room at the top."
Margaret Thatcher

"There is no substitute for hard word."
Thomas Edison

"Make yourself indispensable, and you will move up. Act as though you are indispensable, and you will move out.
Jules Ormont

"God has given us common sense, and He expects us to use it for these small matters."
Catherine Marshall

"Always be in a state of expectancy and see that you leave room for God to come in as He likes."
Oswald Chambers

Chapter 5

BE FLEXIBLE, BE PREPARED AND OPEN TO OPPORTUNITIES

I believe that many people are used to doing things in the same manner and are so set in their ways that they push people away. They are often not willing to hear suggestions about new techniques and miss out on great opportunities, not only to learn and to grow, but to new experiences and the chance to learn about new things.

Are you open to new ideas?

Are you flexible? Would others describe you as being flexible? Why or why not?

Give some examples of your flexibility:

Add some adventure to your life if you are the kind of person who has a fairly set routine -- work, home, church -- work, home, church -- always with the same people at work, home, church. You eat at the same places, shop at the same stores.

These habits are fine. They add certain order to our lives and many people must have a set schedule in order to function.

Would people describe you as rigid? Difficult to work with?

Great leaders, however, explore. They challenge themselves and others and usually have inquisitive minds. They want to talk about the issues related to the business and discuss opportunities for growth, customer service and cost-cutting measures. Great leaders are usually at the head of the line "pushing and pulling" to make sure that they have a team of people with them. They have lots of ideas and it doesn't matter if they have 30 ideas and only 5 worked, because tomorrow they will have 30 more.

Their brains are always working. They are the kind of people who keep a pad by the side of the bed because they get ideas in the middle of the night. I am one of those people. Some of my best ideas for services for children, fund raising and community partnerships as well as adjusting organizational procedures have come to me during the middle of the night. I also have the benefit of working with others who generate ideas, so the atmosphere is lively and creative. Work to contribute to such an environment!

I want to encourage you to dream and explore. What do I mean by that? It is simply a challenge to evoke the great Star Trek phrase, which is "go where you have never gone before." Go to a new museum, visit an art gallery, drive two hours away from home and see a different neighborhood. Plan a trip to a place you have never visited. Eat new foods and, if you can, take your family members and discuss the new experience. You will begin to expand your world and your thinking will change.

I believe in continuous learning, reading and meeting new people. I have a personal goal of meeting five new people every day -- in meetings -- at church -- on the train -- walking -- in my neighborhood and everywhere. This posture provides a fertile opportunity to listen, learn and grow and supports a great saying I use frequently, "The more places you go, the more you will know and the more you know, the more places you go."

Say it again and adopt it as your own!!!

You must be flexible since big thinkers need to constantly refresh and renew and that means talking with different people and being open to their suggestions and ideas.

Are you open to new ideas? Are you a big thinker?

What is your weekly routine?

When is the last time you visited a different museum or art gallery?

Do you tend to stay in a fairly confined area?

Do you usually socialize with the same people?

Are you always reading the same books, magazines and papers?

Do you think you have had a grand idea?

Have you written it down?

What do you want to do in the next three to five months? Years? How are you going to accomplish this?

Are you prepared for a new opportunity?

In what field or area of interest?

If you don't feel you are prepared for a new field, how will you get prepared? Do you feel you need to go to college or back to college? Do you need to take a course? If the answer is yes to any of the above, get a pen -- and start writing!

What is your first step? THIS IS VERY IMPORTANT!!!

Do you have all of the information about the next steps so that you can make an informed decision?

Write the following and tape it to your telephone, put it over your desk or hang it where you can frequently refer to it:

Four things never come back
- the spoken work
- the arrow speeding from the bow
- the past life
- the neglected opportunity

"You create your opportunities by asking for them."
　　　Patty Hansen

"One of the earliest lessons I learned as a child was that if you looked away from something, it might not be there when you looked back."
　　　John Edgar Wideman

"If Columbus had turned back, no one would have blamed him. Of course, no one would have remembered him either."
　　　Source unknown

"Do not waste a minute -- not a second -- in trying to demonstrate to others the merits of your performance. If your work does not vindicate itself, you cannot vindicate it."
　　　Rev. Thomas Wentworth Higginson

Romans 12:21 Do not be overcome by evil, but overcome evil with good.

Isaiah 40:28 Do you not know? Have you not heard? The Lord is the everlasting God, the Creator of the ends of the earth. He will not grow tired or weary, and his understanding no one can fathom.

II Samuel 22:2-3 And he said, The Lord is my rock and my fortress, and my deliverer; The God of my rock; in him will I trust: he is my shield, and the horn of my salvation, my high tower, and my refuge, my savior; thou savest me from violence.

Psalm 71 In thee, O Lord, do I put my trust; let me never be put to confusion.

> "To worship Him in truth means to worship Him honestly, without hypocrisy, through faith in His word, both living, which is Jesus and written, which is the Bible."
> Anne Graham Lotz

Notes:

Chapter 6

ACKNOWLEDGE THOSE WHO HAVE HELPED YOU

Too many people are quick to take all the credit and never really remember those who helped them along the way. Each of us has had mentors, teachers, parents, friends, co-workers and others who have helped in special ways. Just a gentle reminder - do not forget them.

Make sure you say thank you and acknowledge them in other ways whenever you can. Both of you will be richer for this act of kindness.

One of the great mysteries of life is how people come together to help. Sometime it is quite by accident when one responds to a simple request, bonds are formed, friendships are cemented, and there is mutual respect formed for years, when support and help are given so that one can accomplish his or her goals.

Who has helped you?

How have you acknowledged them?

What have you done to help others?

Make sure you surround yourself with people who truly have your best interests at heart. When we hear that someone has made an unusual decision such as quitting a job (before securing another one), we wonder who in the world has given that person advice and further, why would that kind of advice be taken.

Many people want to give advice, but they simply don't know enough to give you information that would be in your best interests.

Make certain that if you are asking people for help and advice that you also have a "filter system" to weed out the poor information and suggestions and really think through career and personal decisions. Often, when major decisions are made, particularly those made without proper review, careers are derailed and sometimes are never reclaimed.

Don't discount jealousy either. Think carefully about those you seek out to give you advice. When you have achieved a certain level of success, there may be some people you have known for years who do not honestly celebrate your success. There might be individuals in your circle of family and friends who do not really want you to succeed, so proceed with caution when anyone gives you personal or career advice.

How well do you really know that person?

How can you sort through career or personal advice in order to make the best decision?

Remember a Heard truth:

> "Everybody doesn't love you and
> Everybody doesn't want you to succeed."

Repeat that:

> "Everybody doesn't love you and
> Everybody doesn't want you to succeed."
> A Heardism

It might not seem like a nice thing to think, however, when you have worked as long as I have worked and in as many different environments, I have watched or have seen individuals who will manipulate, scheme and connive their way to the head of the line. I have watched a boss (who was married) secretly dating an employee. I, along with other employees, watched that employee get the great (and easy) assignments, when those assignments could have easily gone to someone else who had more seniority and who was more qualified.

The person who does not want you to succeed is not wearing a sign saying, "I don't want to help you." On the contrary, that person might very well portray himself or herself as your great and good friend. This is why it is imperative that you surround yourself with the right people. It is critical that you have someone to talk to who will review your work-related or personal issues -- well before you make a major career or personal decision.

I recommend that you have your spouse or trusted friend review all the facts and then get a pencil and paper and quietly list all of the options. Make certain that the pros and the cons are clear and that you have indicated to the best of your knowledge the implications of each phase of your decision. What is likely to happen if I say "yes" and what will be the reaction if I say "no"? Ultimately, you must decide what is in your best interests and only you and very close, confidential advisers will be able to help you gauge the financial, personal and career implications.

Remember that you need great counsel and keep trying until you have someone who will only want the best for you and will be looking out for your well being and your future.

THE GREAT ASSISTANT

If you are at a management level high enough to have a personal administrative assistant or multiple staff members to help you, remember that it is up to you tell that person/s what you expect and how they can be helpful and how you can help each other. The role of an assistant is just that -- to assist you and help you do a better job. There cannot be a true partnership is there is not good communication.

Tell the assistant your preference regarding everything from how you would like to have the telephone answered to what should be said when you are at a meeting, out of the building or have stepped away from the desk and are not available.

The unacceptable phrases are:

> "She's not here and I don't know where she is right now."
> "I don't know when she'll be back."
> "I'm not sure and I don't have her schedule."

Or the dreaded, "She's tied up." This brings the picture to mind of someone literally being bound to a chair with heavy rope and unable to move.

With cell phones, e-mail and other technological supports, a system should be confirmed so that you and your assistant have a plan for contacting you and you are comfortable with her responses during your absence.

Some more acceptable responses would be:

> "I'm sorry, she is unavailable, but is there anything I can do to help?"

> "She's not available at the moment, but I'll have her call you as soon as she is available (or as soon as she returns to the office). Is there something I can do in the meantime?"

> "One moment, please, let me see if she's finished the meeting." The call, via cell phone or inter-office, can then be connected.

An assistant should always offer to help and be able to take care of many of the details for the day such as re-confirming dates and times and other information which is related to the schedule.

From confirming the calendar, to setting up meetings, to composing and typing correspondence to writing meeting minutes to organizing and managing various projects, an assistant can be an invaluable extra set of hands and another way to help ease your schedule.

Do you have an assistant? If so, have you reviewed your preferences with him or her?

Are you both clear about the procedures or do you need to periodically review them?

Are you an assistant?

Do you know what is expected of you in the relationship between the two of you?

What are some of the things you focus on during a typical day?

What are some of your questions about your role?

How will you arrange to have these questions answered?

How can you be more supportive?

Make sure that you have found ways to thank your assistant and for the assistant, make sure that you thank your boss as well. It is a two-way street and each of you will perform better the more you support each other.

It is very important that you keep in touch with each other in case of emergencies and also just to keep the flow of paper and information moving during the day even if you are at a meeting and often out of the office. I have found that it is easiest for me to call my assistant every two hours or so when I am away from the office. I prefer this method rather than keeping my cell phone turned on and having it ring at awkward moments.

She is not able to determine if I am in the middle of a discussion, at a critical point in a speech, asking for a large donation, in a large planning meeting, reviewing the advocacy agenda with an elected official or reviewing information with a key volunteer. With the contact system I have established with my assistant, I am in contact within a certain time frame and she knows that she can, and has reached me in an emergency since she is also responsible for confirming my calendar and has appropriate contact information for each day.

You must negotiate a great relationship as well.Make sure you are both clear about what is expected and your preferences. It may take a few tries to find out what is most comfortable, but the result will be well worth the effort.

Once you have established a routine, make sure to review it every few months and be willing to adjust when your schedule or the workload dictates that a change is necessary. Remember, be flexible.

HOW LONG? ONE STEP AT A TIME!!!

After college, I continued my career as an Executive Secretary. I had been working during high school and after high school as a Secretary. Next, I went to a business/secretarial school and then to college where I received an Associate's Degree in Executive Secretarial Studies, so I know what it means to be a great (notice I did not say good) assistant. Yes, I am going to push you to have that kind of confidence. No, not in an arrogant manner, just a simple acknowledgment that you have performed well and others have also confirmed this. Do your best!!!

I wasn't always in that chair in the corner office. I have worked at administrative posts and in line positions, a diversified business (and have for over 20 years) and have served as a consultant to many national groups.

As my career progressed and I completed a Bachelor's Degree then a Master's Degree and after working several more years, completed a post-graduate seminar, so I knew the value a great assistant could bring to my office. As an aside, from start to finish, the "college" part of my formal education took 17 years, so I know a little about "one step at a time" and "one course at a time" and HAVING A GOAL AND A BIG DREAM.

Whichever title you have, either assistant or supervisor/boss, do your best to have a great working schedule and supportive relationship. You can learn from each other.

What is working really well and needs to be celebrated and continued?

What do you need to change?

As a part of the schedule, you should have some sense of how much time you spend on the telephone, particularly if you have a position where you have a high volume of outside calls. You also need to review how much time you are spending in meetings. You must have time "at your desk" for the administrative matters of your position.

In this instance, such as mine, your assistant needs to have enough confidence and authority to take some of the calls and complete the request, with the understanding that you two have reviewed your preferences in terms of how requests should be handled.

This is an ongoing process and needs constant attention because each call is different. Good judgement needs to be exercised and a pleasant manner displayed at all times. After all, your assistant is representing you.

Numbers 4:23 "From thirty years old and upward until fifty years old shalt thou number them; all that enter in to perform the service, to do the work in the tabernacle of the congregation."

"Associate yourself with men of good quality, if you esteem your own reputation; for it is better to be alone than in bad company."

George Washington

"The Bible is not only infallible in its totality, but it is inerrant in all its parts. The writer of Proverbs says it well: Every word of God is pure. He is a shield to those who put their trust in Him."

John MacArthur, Jr.

"Father, your love never ceases. Never. Though we spurn you, ignore you, disobey you, you will not change. Our evil cannot diminish your love. Our goodness cannot increase it. Our faith does not earn it anymore than our stupidity jeopardizes it. You don't love us less if we fail. You don't love us more if we succeed. Your love never ceases."

Max Lucado

Talk about great assistants, I worked with some of the best in the business. I have worked with Janet Elliott, Marjorie Jordan and Phyllis Schwartz in Connecticut and Linda Giles, Debbie Cutter and Ann Guy in Massachusetts. Thank you all.

HAVE A GREAT SENSE OF HUMOR AND LEARN TO REALLY PLAY AND RELAX WITH THOSE YOU LOVE

Throughout your daily schedule, learn to laugh. No matter what, unless it is a very personal tragedy for someone else, you can probably see the humor in almost every situation. Be able to relax enough and comfortable enough to laugh at yourself.

Take vacation time and "mental health" days. Learn to plan ahead so that you can spend happy times with your family and also allow time just for yourself. We always seem to find time to attend funerals and wakes.

We have established something in our family called, "The Magic Memory" weekend, and it is just that. A time to relax together, at a small hotel where we wear casual clothes, sit and visit, walk and talk and have meals together. We include our children and and their wives and our grandchildren as well the in-laws, so everyone has their primary family members for this special time.

We take lots of pictures, play games and read. Each person also brings several special gifts, so there is a huge drawing and everyone, including the children, gets to pick the presents they will take home. It indeed does create "Magic Memories."

Know some funny stories that you can share in mixed company. Remember humorous meetings or social events that you have attended. These occasions often become part of the family or company's "lore" and for years to come, the laughter will begin as soon as someone says, "Do you remember when..." and the gales of laughter will follow. Enjoy your family and associates and relax enough to laugh often and celebrate your gift of joy.

Notes:

Chapter 7

BE ON TIME

Yes, this is a basic concept, but it warrants space here.

Remember it's the little things.

Are you the kind of person who arrives at work on time?

Are you often the last person to arrive? Are you often late or always late?

Do you find yourself constantly rushing in the morning and not able to quickly settle into your work routine once you arrive at the office?

What can you do to break the habit of being late?

What can you do to plan your schedule better?

What can you do to eliminate rushing in the morning?

My daily schedule often starts with early morning meetings (yes, often starting at 6 or 7a.m.) and during the fall campaign when we are raising millions for our community and neighborhood programs; we will frequently need to be at a hotel for a meeting by 5 a.m.

After this early start to my day, my schedule doesn't end at 5 or 6 p.m., but often also includes a dinner, an award program, planning meeting, community volunteer salute or a speech in support of one of our member agencies or when one of our key donors or board members is getting an award or I am on the program to "roast or toast" a donor or key volunteer.

Yes, this is quite a schedule for me, and yet, part of who I am is that I am on time. People know that about me. I am on time.

I am precise and I encourage you to develop that reputation as well. Try to start earlier and make certain that you are allowing enough time to commute, park or walk and, with ever-increasing frequency; navigate each building's security requirements.

In this instance, as in earlier chapters, remember you have to have a plan, and you have to be prepared. You also to have discipline and energy. More about guarding your energy later in the Personal Side of Leadership Chapter.

Just like the schedule in your old school days, I recommend the following for the chronically tardy. These are simple rules and you might think they are extremely basic, (and they are), but stop and think about all the people you know who are habitually late and who always keep you and others waiting. With these facts in mind, this list might come in handy for you share with the offenders:

- go to bed at least 30 minutes earlier
- finish as much as possible the night before
- lay out your clothes (but only after checking the hems, etc.)
- put anything you must take by the door (or put in the car)
- set the breakfast table
- finish as much as possible for others (lunches for children, etc.)
- before you go to bed, set two alarm clocks if you are sleeping through the first one
- check the gas on the way home and not in the morning
- carefully review train/bus schedules since they might have changed or the route might have been extended and thus arrive at your stop or final destination a little later (or earlier)

- sit in your car and relax before you start the car and take three deep breaths. This will make your morning drive much calmer.

Being on time adds to your reputation and enhances your credibility. Remember that it's the little things. Don't eliminate yourself.

BE READY, BE READY, BE READY!!!

Are you precise?

What do you do to keep on schedule and be on time?

What can you do to ease your schedule?

Being on time also projects confidence and determination. These are two qualities leaders need and those who work with you and for you will watch you. Setting the example of being on time will tell others that you are a serious person and that you understand that it is "rude to be perpetually late."

Being on time shows respect for others. After all, when you rush in late, even a few minutes late, it means that you did not think that the people you were meeting with were important enough to get there on time. It also tells your staff that this is acceptable behavior. Think what your organization would look like and think about the odds of achieving your goals if you could not depend on anyone or at least the majority of the employees to ever get to work on time.

The habit of being tardy often slips into other areas of the business. If you don't start work on time, does that also mean that the project does not have to finish on time? Don't you think that employees will model your behavior and ask, "do we really have to finish that project on time?" If you, as the leader, are always late, does that mean that every employee can come and go whenever he or she pleases? Order will quickly turn to chaos and you will have a very difficult time getting your reputation back if the first phrase used to describe you is, "She's a great person," however, the second phrase, is "yes, but she is always late."

I remember a time, in the not too distant past, when most people would politely laugh about a person who was always late. It would be common and often acceptable behavior. It was accepted or even tolerated because that person had a great personality and/or was a vital contributor to the organization or, with personal relationships, is a dear friend.

In recent times, I have seen that dramatically changed. Being late is no longer a joke. Being late is not cute. I don't believe there is any such thing as being fashionably late. If you are late, you are late. Being late is not considered a great characteristic. If you constantly have to explain why you are late, pledge to eliminate that from your routine.

Don't eliminate yourself.

Remember that the little things can make a big difference.

Do you prioritize so that you can eliminate some obligations?

Are you organized at work?

Are you organized at home?

Are you trying to do too much and can't say "no?" Read this question out loud!!!

Do you plan enough quiet time to get organized and schedule properly?

What are you doing to adjust your schedule to work on being on time?

What can you do to foster a more precise work environment?

What can you eliminate in your schedule to make your life calmer?

Psalms 145:14 The Lord upholdeth all that fall, and raiseth up all those that he bowed down.

Luke 5:16 He withdrew himself into the wilderness and prayed.

"People do not lack strength: they lack will."
Victor Hugo

"I know! I am certain! There is the great Christian note: facing life at its very worst, yet there is no fear, no uncertainty. There is no shrinking or trembling, as you look at this unknown future. Not at all! What ever it may be, I am confident! I am persuaded! I am certain! I am sure."
Martyn Lloyd-Jones

"Always have a plan and believe in it. Nothing happens by accident."
Chuck Knox

Luke 12:35-40 Be dressed and always ready for service and keep your lamps burning, like men waiting for their master to return from a wedding banquet, so that when he comes and knocks they can immediately open the door for him. You also must be ready, because the Son of Man will come at an hour when you do not expect Him.

70

Ephesians 5:15-16 Be very careful, then, how you live - not as unwise but as wise, making the most of every opportunity, because the days are evil.

Notes:_____

Chapter 8

LEARN HOW TO SELL YOUR IDEA AND YOURSELF - BE
PERSUASIVE!!!

Do you have a great attitude? Are you persuasive?

An idea, no matter how great it is needs a salesperson to explain it
to those who will be asked to help make it a reality. You need to
practice your message and work hard at being persuasive. Some
people find this easier than others. If you are a born salesperson,
you are lucky. If not, you have to practice, practice, practice.

If you have to work too hard at being persuasive, it will show. You
must be sincere and project your belief in what you are saying. Do
not try to fake a position. People know that right away that you not
being sincere. Make sure that you are being true to yourself and yet
I want to push you to stretch and try new things. If you have always
been quiet, learn to speak up. If you have never proposed an idea,
write it down, hone it until it is clear and precise and then review it
with a trusted friend who is not involved with the group where the
idea will be proposed.

Expand your thinking and test the waters. Try to reach and risk.
Successful people have failed many times, often tried ideas that
haven't worked, but the odds have been in their favor because they
have not been timid about trying new things. If you are struggling
with this, try new ideas at church groups, in family settings and at
work. Don't be put off by people who dismiss your ideas automatically. They need to get used to hearing you and seeing you in a
new confident role. Practice.

Do you have an idea you want to propose? Write it here? Practice
saying it!

Sometimes, if the idea is so important to you and you are passionate about it, that feeling will surface and the audience or your co-workers will feel your message as well as hear it.

You would be well served if you exhibit great energy. People respond to energy, precision and passion. You will need not only great energy, but stamina as well. You can have a quick burst of energy for a short-term project, but do you have stamina for the long term?

What do people say about your energy? What would you say about your energy and stamina?

Are you a disciplined person?

Are you passionate about your work?

Is there a cause for which you have a deep commitment?

Do you have a written communications plan about selling your idea?

How will you keep people up to date?

What kind of help will you need?

Where will you get the help?

How will you evaluate the response to your idea, how well you have communicated and how people reacted to your idea or plan?

Your idea needs momentum. It is very important to have early success and report that success to all those who have been involved. You need to incorporate that message of success (or progress, as I like to call movement toward the finish line).

Remember to be honest. If there are problems, find the appropriate forum for a complete review. Again, make sure that you have all the facts. Make certain that you have complete and current information and that you or a trusted deputy has checked the accuracy of the data.

Are you technologically savvy? What does that mean? The answer is different for each of us.

I don't spend all day talking in bytes and megahertz since I am lucky to have an executive assistant and others who help with clerical support, however, I can operate a computer, write drafts (as I did for the early drafts and final phase of this book and other work), produce documents for the details of my work and access the internet as well as e-mail. That's all I need to do at this point, however, if you want to or need to do other functions, I encourage you to force yourself to make time for continuous training, so that you are as proficient as possible.

The real answer to that question is that technologically savvy means what is appropriate for your company and your position. Are you constantly taking the time of one or two people to get information for you that you could easily access yourself?

Is this a great use of your time or the time of others?

What are the barriers to becoming more proficient?

What are the benefits?

What are the other issues?

What will I need to do to become more proficient? Do I need more training to move in this direction?

Who will help me?

I Joshua 3:18
My little children, let us not love in word, neither in tongue, but in deed and in truth.

Psalm 120:2
Deliver my soul, O Lord; from lying lips and from a deceitful tongue.

> "When we compare our wisdom with God's, we find that we are simple and dull in relation. We have neither the experience of God, nor the insight. His knowledge so far exceeds our own that we seem naïve and inept. Luckily, God offers His wisdom and knowledge with no strings attached... He only wants us to avoid the pitfalls that come our way. Christian maturity comes when we can admit that we need help and accept the aid God so freely offers."
>
> Dan and Nancy Dick

In many instances, it is necessary for leaders to exhibit forcefulness. You will often need to assert yourself. You need to be decisive and sometimes make really tough decisions. You will also be called upon to inspire and motivate others. This might be true at home, at work or at church. If you are a volunteer in your community and sit on a committee or a board, you will need these qualities as well.

Also, you will be expected to mentor, coach and train as well as be a sensitive and attentive listener. While we will spend some time in this book about making great presentations and speeches, I cannot emphasize enough how important it is for you to be a great listener as well.

I have worked hard at being a great listener and people have responded. I am able to convey a quiet and open posture and this encourages a conversation that will often elicit very personal information -- information that everyone knows I will take to my grave.

A leader will often be asked to hear about personal and very private problems, particularly if the problems are effecting attendance and/or performance. When tragedy strikes, the leader is often the one to give comfort, particularly if the tragedy has happened to an employee or the family member of an employee. The leader must listen and then convey the sensitive information to key employees or sometimes the entire workforce.

You will be able to gauge the pulse of the organization if you have been a careful listener. I am a listener in the office corridors and in the ladies room, yes, that is where some of the most helpful information is exchanged, because employees seize the opportunity for a few minutes with me and I stop and listen.

I have made it a rule; however, never to discuss business in any elevator since you do not know the relationships or affiliations of the other occupants. You could be discussing information that would be totally inappropriate. Also, those hearing your conversation would certainly wonder that "if they are talking about Y and X today, they may be talking about me tomorrow." The message here is very clear, be a sensitive listener and be sensitive about where you hold your conversations and talk about others.

A word about sustainability. Your employees and those around you who are looking to you for leadership must feel that you have sustainability. Do you plan to see the project to its expected completion date? Can you take the questions, criticisms and challenges and still sustain the momentum?

Momentum is important. Remember that the only success we know of that comes from sitting still -- comes from a hen.

Are you forceful enough to win over the critics and win other converts as well? Do you have the will to win?

Do you know that you have the will to win?

What are the other qualities you possess which speak to determination?

What do you need to do to strengthen this area?

Who can help you?

We are in a very fast-paced era and technology means that the evening news can have a live report about activity on half a world away and we are bombarded with information through cell phones, pagers, palm pilots and other devices. Some of our cars have phones and we are connected to office systems at our homes and lap tops and compact DVD players allow the constant flow of news, information and entertainment. Most people are on data overload.

We hear and have to process so much information, that we need to make certain that we have appropriate filters and store and use just what we need. We also have to find quick ways to retrieve information so that current data is available prior to decision making.

In this competitive environment, those who have strong communication skills who also possess the characteristics of determination, passion and flexibility will certainly have the advantage over the leader who does not fit this description.

> "He who is not courageous enough to take risks will accomplish nothing in life."
> Anonymous

> "This is no time for ease and comfort. It is the time to

dare and endure."
Winston Churchill

"Never allow another person's opinion to be your goal. They may not like you."
Bishop T.D. Jakes

Believe in yourself. After all, the Ark was built by amateurs and volunteers and the Titanic was built by experts!!!

"Effort only fully releases its reward after a person refuses to quit."
Napoleon Hill

"The prime function of a leader is to keep hope alive."
John W. Gardner

"We can do anything we want to do if we stick to it long enough."
Helen Keller

"In tenderness He sought me, weary and sick with sin. And on His shoulders brought me, back to his fold again!"
W. Spence Walton

Chapter 9

LEARN HOW TO NEGOTIATE

Leaders need to know how to negotiate. You will not always get what you want or need right away. Sometimes you are in a position just to sign a purchase order, call and make a request or, if you own the business, simply give an instruction.

In other positions, you might have the authority to get simple yet important things like supplies. (Difficulty getting supplies won't seem so simple if you have to almost jump through hoops to get them.) You might have to negotiate if the order is for a large and, or expensive piece of equipment, rather than a few pads and pens.

If you are placing a large order, you might have to have an extended conversation about everything from the price, to the model number of the equipment, the service information, any warranties, the delivery schedule and whether or not the old equipment will be picked up as a part of this transaction. You might have to negotiate.

If you are the manager and want to attend a special conference and have already been alerted that the training budget has been reduced, you will definitely have to negotiate.

After you have been working at the same company for several years and have had great performance appraisals, you might feel that you deserve more money. If the raise has not been automatically given, you will have to negotiate.

There are many instances every day when we negotiate. We usually don't give that conversation such a formal title, but we are truly negotiating. If you are purchasing a new car, this is the classic site of negotiations. You may not know it, however, but every time you get your hair cut and styled, you have to do a bit of negotiating. The stylist usually wants to cut your hair a little shorter and you find yourself in a quiet contest of wills.

If you get in a cab and want to go a certain way, the driver might not want to go that way, citing construction or any other excuse. Be firm. Negotiate? Not!

An employee asks for more time off because of a personal problem and you have to weigh that request against the time already taken and the work needs as well as the morale of your organization and other employee needs as well.

If you are married or have a significant other, you are probably a pretty good negotiator. If you have survived teenage children, you are no doubt an excellent negotiator.

Use the skills you have gained from your everyday life to become an even better negotiator. The first rule of this art (and it is an art) is to try very hard to remain calm. Always be prepared not to get what you want and have that alternate strategy ready. Practice and write it down.

The next suggestion is to be very clear about what you want and perhaps the most important basic element in any negotiation, is to know what you are willing to give up to get what you really want.

Are you are good negotiator?

What is the one thing that you want now?

Are you willing to negotiate for it?

What are you willing to give up?

Is it important for you to win or are you working toward a win-win situation so that you and the other party are both happy?

How will you negotiate?

Where and when (since the setting is often a key to success).

If it is a serious matter, you can use a neutral space. If you want to take the upper hand, use your office. If you are only willing to negotiate so far, almost any space will do.

Remember to determine ahead of time what is really important and what you are willing to give up.

Who will help you?

> "People are always blaming their circumstances for what they are. I don't believe in circumstances. The people who get on in the world are the people who get up and look for the circumstances they want and if they can't find them, they make them."
> George Bernard Shaw

> "Right is right, even if everyone is against it and wrong is wrong, even if everyone is for it."
> William Penn

> "An invincible determination can accomplish almost anything and in this lies the great distinction between great men (and women) and little men (and women).
> Thomas Fuller

> "What makes us religious people is not the church we attend, not the Bible we read, not even our good deeds. The only thing, finally, that makes us religious is our relationship with God."
> Statement from "The Upper Room" publication

You will not succeed every time you approach a situation where you are asking for something or something special is being asked of you. Make sure that you keep your emotions under control and always have an alternate approach. Sometimes you might be faced with a long (let's stay here until we can settle this) negotiation session. You need to really plan for all the potential options which are presented and also have a strategy to "leave the room if it is appropriate" to give yourself thinking time. You have to plan, plan and plan again prior to participating in a critical session when long-term changes will probably occur as a result of the decisions reached in the negotiation session.

Again, be prepared and read every detail that is available to you prior to attending the meeting.

Notes:

Chapter 10

LEARN TO SAY "NO" AND LEARN HOW TO DELEGATE

It is very flattering to be called on to do special projects or to be told that you are the one that "must" be on that program at church or it just won't be the same.

You might be the person that every member of the family leans on and expects you to run to them whenever they call.

You could be the employee who is always asked to do special projects and, if you happen to be single, is never asked if indeed you have special plans around the holiday season.

Perhaps you don't even wait for someone to call you, you simply volunteer.

A few times a year, you might say that you feel STRESSED OUT. In fact, there is a bumper sticker that reads, "I am woman, I am invincible, I am exhausted."

Women are often struggling with multiple titles (and yes, many men are as well) and all too often, new ones get added to the list weekly. You are the daughter, the wife, the mother, the neighbor, the grandmother, the available friend, the employee or the owner or the CEO or the secretary or the aide or the associate or the team member. You have often made sacrifices that you never thought you would have to make simply because you have not learned how to say "no," to delegate or to negotiate.

Whatever your work title or how many of the other titles fit your current situation, I probably haven't listed all of them and they don't completely cover what you are being asked to do at work and at home. There is not one of your titles that addresses the multiple roles you are playing.

Sleep is at a premium. Time for exercise, reading, relaxing, enjoying your family has somehow gotten lost.

You must find a way to phase out of some of your obligations and have more personal time and more thinking time. I know from experience that you have to be very strong and learn to delegate some of the activities. If you have a staff member who wants to learn new skills, he or she is the appropriate person to mentor and transfer some of your work projects. If you are not the manager or the supervisor, this will take some negotiation and, in fact, might not even be possible depending on your work situation. If you are constantly frustrated, think about the kind of work you are doing and whether or not you want to continue in this position. If you went back to school, would additional education make a difference at your organization or company? Can I adjust my work schedule? Each of these things should be reviewed if you are chronically exhausted, short-tempered and running out of time most days before you complete your personal and family obligations.

If you have the ability to move some of the projects from your "in box" then do so. If you have some options about a work schedule, then review them. If you can adjust some of your obligations at church or home or in the community, then adjust them.

If you do not, you must sort out some of the personal and family requests you have been asked to do and start to say no.

It requires practice. You must respond that "you thank them so much for thinking about you, however, you already have a commitment." You need not explain what it is, just say you cannot go or do or speak or meet or bake or drive or whatever the request covers and hold your ground.

Practice. Practice. Practice!!! You can just say "no, thank you," but you need to say "no" more than "yes" so that you get some balance back in your life.

When is the last time you read a book for enjoyment?

What are some things on your to do list that you are going to delegate to someone else?

Who can help?

How will you control your reactions (saying "no" more than saying "yes") when your family members or others make constant requests for your time?

When will you say no?

How will you say no?

Practice, practice, practice.

Think of determination like the cartoon character, Wile E. Coyote. He chases the Roadrunner, a very smart bird. The bird stops and the coyote tries, but cannot stop. He runs into brick walls and mountains and yet he never gets hurt. True, this is a cartoon character, but we have to admire his grit and will. He is invincible. He never gets hurt and the falls don't ever faze him.

He gets back up and begins a new chase. The stacks of ACME dynamite explode and yet he continues to run. The painting on a wall appears like a tunnel and so he runs as fast as he can and slams into the side of a building, instead of going through what looks like a tunnel. With all of his energy, he fails to catch the Roadrunner. No matter what happens, dynamite blasts, falls, trains running over him and flattening him like a pancake, he gets back up and back in the race. You have to admire this character. He will not give up and when he is down, his only thought is how to get back up. Does this describe you?

How do you handle adversity?

How many times have you felt like "giving up," particularly after you have hit that brick wall? If you haven't given up, congratulate yourself. If you have overcome some very serious obstacles, give yourself lots of credit!!! This book is to challenge, but it is also meant to celebrate what you have accomplished.

"I don't know the key to success, but the key to failure is trying to please everybody."
Bill Cosby

"It does not take much strength to do things, but it requires great strength to decide what to do."
Elbert Hubbard

Matthew 6:32-34 For the pagans run after all these things, and your heavenly Father knows that you need them, But seek first his kingdom and his righteousness, and all these things will be given to you as well. Therefore, do not worry about tomorrow, for tomorrow will worry about itself. Each day has enough trouble of its own.

MAKE SURE THAT YOU KEEP YOUR FINANCIAL HOUSE IN ORDER.

The headlines of the past several years have highlighted more than a few CEO's, CFO's and accountants who have not followed the rules. Many have certainly enjoyed lavish lifestyles and, until the public was aware of all of the details, they flew in private jets, maintained several homes, waterfront retreats and city apartments. In addition, they acquired millions of dollars of artwork, commissioned sculptures and worked in extravagant office suites. Their cars and boats were specially ordered and their homes boasted five and six garages.

They routinely added millions of dollars to their own bonuses and -- with help from other members of the executive team -- awarded themselves millions more through stock options and other perks. We have since learned that most all of their living expenses were covered by company funds and those who were shareholders, in effect, paid for some of these expenses. For the publicly traded companies, new rules are being proposed that will help to eliminate many of these things and we now know that people within these companies knew about most of what was happening.

Your lifestyle might not be anywhere near what I have cited above. You might live very modestly, trade in your car only when it can't go another mile, have made regular deposits to your savings and other accounts and are on target with your retirement investments and plans. Careful use of money is what happens to most people, however, this section is for those who are perpetually over-extended. This is for those who are in debt, always shopping, always needing to have "things" and desperately trying to "keep up with the elusive Joneses."

Money problems -- being in debt -- gambling -- these are things which can often cause us to make poor decisions and still more inappropriate choices. Just a caution here to watch your finances. Granted, some of us are better than others, but remember that at certain executive levels in companies, you might be asked to share your credit report. You will also need to make sure that your finances are in order if you have to get a home mortgage, re-finance your home or have the need for emergency loans for personal or family issues. Make sure to watch your finances and make decisions, which will give you a more secure retirement.

Notes:

Chapter 11

MAKE SURE YOU HAVE PLANNING AND QUIET THINKING TIME

How many times have you asked yourself, "how did I get myself into this situation?"

You might have had great intentions and had originally planned something else, but in the rush of the day or the timing of the meeting, your decision has resulted in a dramatic turn of events. You have now found yourself with a commitment to do something that you really don't want to do. Your schedule of work, family and personal obligations has left you very little time for yourself and you question yourself and the wisdom of your decision. The weight of your schedule can mean that you are feeling angry, frustrated and disappointed.

If you are at this point in your life, it might be because you have not taken enough planning time and quiet thinking time. Both of these are necessary for great leadership. We spoke about discipline earlier, well, here it is again!

Planning time will allow you to think about your schedule, the current and future projects you want to work on as well as the challenges in your business life. Planning time will also provide an opportunity for you to write (and I do recommend writing down the elements which you need to review so that key elements are not forgotten) about options, timing and issues and questions about any special projects or your future plans.

You cannot worry, for the first time, about the total income and the total expenses of your budget and what will appear on the bottom line and whether or not you are over or under your budget on December 31st, if that is the day your fiscal year closes.

The day to start worrying about the bottom line is on January 1st, so that you will have the opportunity to make any necessary adjustments. This is also true in your personal world.

Let's have a hypothetical situation:

> Your boss advises that he has a new committee related to a scheduled move for your company and he wants you to be the Chairman of the Committee. He says, "it is a simple task," but he needs someone who can make sure that all the details are taken care of and you are skilled at checking all of the details. You have a brief conversation in the hall and about an hour later your boss comes to your desk and brings you a folder with some notes about the move.

> You are now the Chairman and "Own" this New Building Project. You have inherited it from someone else.

> The Project is very important since it will involve the relocation of over 500 people to a new office complex. The budget for the move has been set at $555,000 and will include confirming moving vans, notifying staff about the schedule for the move, working with the appropriate companies to secure information and getting confirmations that all of the utilities will be turned on prior to the move. Also, you are responsible for working with a committee of four people. The committee meets every week and each member of the team has been asked to take the lead regarding one component related to the move.

> Sounds simple, however, you have realized that you are not familiar with the details of a move and have incurred a problem because the company wants to use a union trucking company for the move and they only notified you about this after you had signed the contract for a non-union company. Your company has now received a notice from the union asking for a meeting and issuing a threat that they will set up picket lines.

Two of the committee members have now called to say that they have conflicts and will not be able to attend your meetings. Your boss has asked to see you and two of the three utility companies have advised that they cannot turn the power on in time to meet your deadline.

An added dimension is that the move has been confirmed for the first Saturday of next month and that is the day of your son's first Little League game. You had promised him you would attend because you missed last year's Opening Day Celebration because you also had to work.

Ask yourself a few questions about this situation.

Did you ask enough questions about this project?

Did you check your calendar to review the date of your son's game?

What can you do about the committee membership?

What can you do now?

What will you try to negotiate?

What happened here that provides lessons about your schedules?

Review this example and ask yourself what you would have done. What might have happened, if time had been taken after the meeting in the hall to quickly check your schedule? If all the key business, personal and family commitments were on the calendar, the information about the baseball game and other things would have been noted.

If you had questions about the Project, you would have called your boss and asked for some "face time" rather than accepting the assignment just on the basis of a brief hallway conversation. Granted, you might not always have a choice about work assignments, but when we dissect this example, there are opportunities to make the situation better for you -- the company -- and your family.

Have you ever worked with someone who has a habit of "dropping" projects in your lap without adequate explanations?

What do you do?

Follow this example and review another option. You could have used the time immediately after you returned to your desk to check not only your calendar, but to take a quiet minute to review your current plans and future commitments and had a strategy in mind for a more thoughtful response.

You always have to weigh the implications of either negotiating a project (reminding your boss that you have just completed a project -- or -- as noted in this example -- lack of familiarity with the issue.) Some would say this would have been a great learning experience. However, it is now obvious that the person who had the project prior to its re-assignment left a lot of details unconfirmed, hence the current problems.

You need quiet thinking time to carefully assess your next moves. You need to have an idea -- at all times -- about some of the key things on your personal and family calendar which might pose a major conflict. You also need to be aware of your own limitations.

Many women have a very difficult time saying no. Not all women, but many women. Why, because we are daughters and want to please our parents. We are wives and want to get an A in that category as well. You get the picture. We are nurturers and helpers.

Also, some women have not had enough experience or practice in negotiating, so I want you to make certain that you continue to review the strategies outlined in this book about your own planning, your own goals and your own schedule so that you are better prepared when someone asks you to do something, go somewhere or participate in a project or on a committee.

Take that quiet time to reflect on your accomplishments, the immediate issues on your calendar and the long-term goals and objectives.

How will you build in quiet time in your life?

Why is quiet/thinking time important for me?

Do your short-term goals compliment your long-term goals?

Are your short-term goals on target?

How will you move to the next level to continue to challenge yourself?

Do you have a plan for the next steps?

Have you thought about what you want to do in your personal and professional life in the next three to five years?

Do you know what you must negotiate to make sure your plan succeeds?

Who will help you?

What else do you need to do to prepare to get ready?

What are some of the obstacles?

How will you overcome the obstacles?

How often do you review your goals?

Who knows about your goals --- and your dreams?
The planning and quiet thinking time are critical and will help you manage your time better. Setting aside time every day will also help keep you balanced. You might use the time to review your calendar.

Is your calendar up to date?

Have you listed all of your business, personal and family obligations?

What can you change?

What can you eliminate?

Another few tips about quiet time. Quiet time is just that -- it is quiet time. It is not in front of the television. It is not in a restaurant. It is not with friends or family members. It is not with your spouse or significant other and it is not with children or grandchildren.

If you are employed full time outside of the house, working part-time, or are semi or completely retired, you will definitely need quiet time and planning and thinking time. This is really a gift for you. With the crush and the speed of data and noise in our lives, we very rarely just take time to sit quietly and reflect on the day, plan for the next day and concentrate on what we want to do in the future.

Quiet thinking and planning time is like a sparking diamond and it will truly bring light into your life. Give yourself that gift!

Use the time to review whether or not you have taken care of those things on your "to do" list. Use the time to make certain that you have a plan to address critical issues in your life. Take time to schedule medical appointments and personal care appointments. These things are not only very important for most people, they are critical for people leading very busy and no doubt, stressful lives. Take time to pray. Make sure that you speak to the Master and thank Him for the blessings in your life. You may not have all you think you need, but we all know that God will provide, we need only ask.

Quiet your life and your schedule long enough to reflect on what you want in your world at work, in your marriage, for yourself and for your future. Make sure that you know what you really want to do and that what you are being asked to do will continue to challenge you and give you a sense of accomplishment. Reflect on the things you have learned while you have been working as well on that very critical "next steps" list.

What have you learned?

Have you improved a skill?

Are there other opportunities for growth and development?

Do you think that your salary is appropriate for your level of responsibilities?

If not, do you have a plan to address this issue?

In your quiet time, have you found a way to adjust your schedule?

Have you been able to prioritize your obligations?

What have you been able to eliminate?

II Chronicles 19:3
Nevertheless there are good things found in thee, in that thou hast taken away the groves out of the land, and has prepared thine heart to seek God.

II Chronicles 20:33
Howbeit the high places were not taken away: for as yet the people had not prepared their hearts unto the God of their fathers.

Revelations 21:6
And the woman fled into the wilderness, where she hath a place prepared of God, that they should feed her there a thousand two hundred (and) threescore days.

> "Little minds are tamed and subdued by misfortune; but great minds rise above them."
> Washington Irving

> "It's already gone wrong, you just don't know it."
> Compton's Law (hanging on the author's wall)

> "The more you know, the less you need to say."
> John Rohn

PERSONAL RESPONSIBILITY - BEING RESILIENT - SOLVING PROBLEMS

The issue for many of us is to make certain that we are able to bounce back. We need to be resilient. We need to be able to "roll with the punches" and exhibit a flexible personality. The fact that we erred does not mean that we will always make a mistake. We need to learn from all of our decisions and make certain that we have reviewed the situation, the request, our schedule and the implications of saying "yes" or saying "no."

A word here about responsibility. When we make a mistake, we need to simply say, "I made a mistake." When we have reported the incorrect information, we need to say; "I misspoke." Whenever we make a mistake, we need to say "I'm sorry" and the most important part of the acknowledgment, of the apology, is that it is done quickly and sincerely!

You will also need to learn how to examine your mistakes. Was it because you were in a hurry?

Did you not understand something?

Were you overextended?

Did you apologize?

How was your apology received?

What can you do to avoid the same mistake again?

What have you done to prepare yourself to respond to requests?

Are you comfortable saying "no?"

What have you declined in the last 30 days?

How did you feel?

What are you doing to better manage your commitments? This is important because mistakes are often made because people are overextended and didn't have enough quiet time to plan how they were going to accomplish all of the things they had agreed to do.

Have you found a way to schedule the critical quiet thinking time?

How often will you take time to think?

Can you list the possible benefits of having thinking time?

The quiet time will arm you with the skills needed to handle difficult decisions as well as the unknown. Quiet time and planning time are important and should be a key part of your weekly agenda.

There are 168 hours in a week. Take one of those hours and invest it in yourself. Your world will function better because of your commitment to this process.

Genesis 18:4
Let a little water, I pray you, be fetched, and wash your feet and rest yourselves under the tree.

Mark 6:31
And He said unto them, come ye yourselves apart into a desert place and rest a while: for there were many coming and going and they had no leisure so much as to eat.

Exodus 33:14
And He said, My presence shall go (with thee) and I will give thee rest.

"There is as much dignity in plowing a field as in writing a poem."
Booker T. Washington

"Speak in love. Do not be judgmental or accusatory."
Rev. Billy Graham

Notes:

Chapter 12

THE ART OF EXECUTION

ACTION - ANNOUNCING YOUR PLANS AND PROGRESS

GETTING STARTED - TAKING THE FIRST STEP

DON'T MAKE IT COMPLICATED!

In the world of work, the announcement of new plans creates some excitement, but that will pale when you announce that you have achieved a key element of your plan. Get started. Make that first decision and act.

Make sure that you think through action steps. Movement. Accomplishment. Action.

You will have a better chance at succeeding at whatever you attempt if you can quickly complete a part of your plan. When you are planning a meeting, as soon as the date, time and place are confirmed, you will feel that you have had movement and so will the other people involved. When you complete the agenda, you will again feel that movement, that action, the completion of a phase of your effort.

If you are planning to have speakers as a part of your meeting, the announcement of the speakers will again create a feeling of excitement and movement. You must make certain that as you complete a part of your plan, you also a plan to inform people about your progress or success.

You will continue to gain credibility and those around you will know that you are serious about your work. Others will begin to confirm and also re-confirm that you are indeed the kind of person who "gets things done. You will have a reputation as one who can get people to the "finish line."

Others will say:

> "She got the ship to the shore."
> "She really pushed the ball over the goal line."
> "She's on the ball."
> "She's a real go-getter."
> "Have her organize the meeting and it'll surely be a good one."
> "Wow, she's really making progress."

You can have the same situation and not have a communications strategy in mind. Perhaps you have not even considered telling the little details of your efforts, but are waiting until the details about the meeting time, date, place, agenda, guest speakers, and even the menu have been confirmed. However, depending on the culture of your work environment, at least some of the details about what you have been asked to do should be conveyed to those who will be attending the meeting.

You would not want to be working on all of the details of the meeting and receive a call from one of the participants asking, "Are we going to have the meeting or not?"

Take control. Share the information. Make certain that everyone involved or concerned knows what you have confirmed and accomplished.

Without this approach, the comments about you are likely to be:

> "I don't know a thing about the meeting."
> "I have to schedule another meeting and I'm wondering about this one."
> "She's been working on this for a few weeks, I wonder what's happening."
> "She's really slow about finishing things."

Learn and strategize. Listen and learn about the little things related to your world of work. Don't eliminate yourself.

Don't make things too complicated. Make sure you can easily explain your plan, your goals and your objectives. You might be familiar with the phrase, "the elevator speech."

This means that your plan, your goals, your objectives could be explained in an elevator. (While I do not support conversations in elevators because you do not always know who else is riding in the elevator, the phrase is appropriate here.)

Normally, you will be in an elevator less than three minutes. What can you say in that time? Is your idea so complicated that you require a half of an hour or more to explain it? Too complicated. Do you have to have charts and graphs? Often too complicated!!!

Remember that phrase, "elevator speech." More about that later.

Whether you have a position with lots of responsibility or a job with more modest requirements, each job presents an opportunity for you to succeed. You should always remind yourself that success comes one step at a time.

Great cathedrals are built with one piece of granite at a time. A great painting begins with the first brush stroke on the canvas. Every best-selling book begins with the first word. Your trip might begin when you review the map, but that review is meaningless until you start the car and drive down the road.

Whatever you do, you must start.

You must carefully think through your very first step. What will you do?

Have you had a dream to try a new hobby?

What would you like to do?

What is keeping you from doing it?

Who would help you?

Who would not support your efforts?

How are you going to overcome this lack of support?

Have you thought about a different type of work?

What are the barriers?

Who would help you?

Successful people often declare their intentions. This might not be true when leaders plan wars and they want the element of surprise or when a coach wants to try a new strategy, however, for most personal goals and most business goals, your plans have a much better chance at success if others understand them and you have enlisted their help. It is very important, however, that you have taken the appropriate amount of time to think through all of the key elements. Remember, don't declare until you have taken that quiet time and planned for many options, but don't wait until you have "perfect conditions." That phrase, "the timing isn't right" has application here. Yes, sometimes the timing is not right. The season is an issue, the money is not available, the people needed are not convinced that the plan will work and you might not have exhibited enough passion, commitment and determination to create excitement about your plans.

Make sure that you have the passion and the will.

Make sure that you are willing to stick with the plan for the long term.

Do you have the will to succeed?

Do you have the energy to win?

When I joined the United Way in Boston in 1992, we were #87 on the large donor list. For gifts of $10,000 and more, donors became members of the deTocqueville Society. We also have giving Societies for those who give at least $1,000 and above.

Imagine being #87? True, there are 1,400 United Way organizations in America, however, I announced in 1992 that I would never print a brochure declaring that we were #87. We wanted to be #1.

Over and over, throughout the community I shared this message. Over and over, to board members, political leaders, donors and non-donors, the service providers who were helping children and youth as well as the elderly. Everyone in Boston knew that I had "waged war" on that goal. I was determined to move up on the list and announced that I wanted to be #1.

We are not as large as New York or had not been growing like the southern cities of Charlotte or Atlanta or even Las Vegas, however, we did not want anyone to miss that we wanted to move up on the list.

Was there a risk? Certainly. Was there a chance that the larger cities of Chicago and Washington, D.C., where they were already collecting significantly larger sums, would make our plan seem foolish? Absolutely.

However, I had a plan. Our board had a plan. The staff had a plan and it was all the same plan. We would target those in our area who had been quite successful during the upbeat Internet years. Even though the Northeast region was the last region to bounce back from the last recession, I felt that we could do it.

Were there doubters? Yes. Did some of the people think we should focus on another strategy? Yes, however, just as I mentioned in the first chapter, I felt I had enough understanding, "buy-in" and acceptance and enough people who could explain the plan. I also felt we had enough people who believed in the United Way, our Board and great staff leaderships and -- me!

What did they see? They saw the passion, the drive, the energy and the focus. Yes, the focus, focus, focus. They also had steady reports of our progress. We moved up to #58, then to #32 and then to #27 and, year by year, with more and more donors willing to support the programs for poor children and their families, we continued to move up on the list.

In the meantime, we paused to celebrate each success, but I also announced that we couldn't rest for long, because we had work to do to continue the momentum.

The progress reports were critical. The acknowledgment of the help of others encouraged those volunteers and staff members as well community leaders who were helping.

In addition, we reported on how important the money was for the critical programs for children.

People felt I had the will, the energy and the determination.

I am happy to report that in March of 2003, we were notified that we were going to receive the award as the #1 city in America for Overall Excellence in our Leadership giving program. Out of eight categories, we were #1 in four categories and our total points for all of our giving programs earned us the #1 ranking.

We had a wonderful celebration. One of our Board members, Martha Crowninshield, was given credit in some brief remarks I made during the celebration for her help in charting this course getting to be #1. She had been the first donor at the $100,000 level in our city and a number of others have since followed, also having previously earned us the distinction of being the #1 city in that category as well. This phase of our work required that I do every single step I am suggesting that you do. This great donor is now one of my dear friends, however, in the early 90's when she first became a donor, she wanted to remain anonymous. She gives and gives very generously to many causes in the Boston region and elsewhere, however she prefers not to have a lot of attention focused on her, but rather on the cause.

It took my planning, strategy, quiet thinking time and negotiating skills to convince her that giving us the ability to print her name would be a key piece to helping us achieve our goals. Initially, her personal preference to remain as a silent donor won out. I was determined. I was persistent (but, in a nice way) and spoke to her again. I told her that her name would be a powerful statement to the community that if she thought our United Way was worthy of gifts that size, then others would be encouraged to give at that level as well.

She was steadfast until she had a chance to review that final argument and yet, true to herself, she wanted to remain as quiet as possible, but allowed that if it would help me and the United Way, she would allow the use of her name.

This was a real breakthrough.

We had the first step. We had the chance for momentum.

Not only did the amount of the gift cause quite a buzz, but the fact that at that point, it was the largest single gift to the annual campaign that we had ever received and it came from a woman. Also, it was a woman who had not been known in the community so there was a bit of mystery about who she was and what she did for a living. Many asked if she had inherited her wealth and when I answered that she had made it the old fashioned way, "she had earned it," the admiration increased ten-fold.

There are others and when they stepped out to be the "first," it was because I was persuasive in getting them to help us launch something very, very special.

I want to pause here and talk about a true visionary. A woman who believes in helping others and who decided to focus on young girls. Jean Temple, also a dear friend, (along with her husband Peter Wilson) helped us to solidify our Initiative called, "Today's Girls...Tomorrow's Leaders" with a major gift. Board members and many spouses have supported, donated, hosted events and their efforts have helped us to achieve the #1 ranking, not just for the deTocqueville Society, but for the Women's Leadership Initiative which supports "Today's Girls...Tomorrow's Leaders" as well.

It is truly magnificent and they and others are listed on my special pages. They all are my heroes and they all are heroes to the thousands of children who will be helped because of their generosity. Leadership in getting everyone on the same page. Yes. Leadership in making sure the staff was motivated. Yes. All of the little things that are written about here were put to good use in making us #1. These things will serve you well -- keep reminding yourself!

A few paragraphs ago I asked you to remember the "elevator speech" phrase.

Here's why. I had to explain the goal of being #1 over and over again. Our staff members had to explain the strategy over and over again. Think about the elevator time - three minutes -- and it was not complicated.

"We're #87 and we want to be #1." That's a very clear goal. Not too complicated. Easy to explain. Not a lot of other information was needed. We are here -- #87 and we want to be there -- at #1. Very clear. Simple.

If the ride had a few more floors to go, you could add, "we're moving with a plan to attract 'high net-worth individuals' and at the same time, work on a strategy to strengthen our corporate and employee giving programs and we need your help and leadership." Not too complicated. Easily understood. Who doesn't want to be #1?

Time that message. Three minutes? Two minutes? It's more like 15 seconds, so we even had time for a brief discussion and a chance to ask our elevator companion to make a donation as well.

Not too complicated.

Small steps.

Take the first step and begin.

Drive. Will. Determination. Energy. Discipline.

Hard work. Yes. A written plan? Yes. Group effort? Yes. All of the elements (and more) that are listed in the first chapter. Develop your plan and continue to keep those involved up to date. Make certain that you make the appropriate adjustments as you proceed so that any challenges are addressed and you stay on course. Don't forget that you won't be successful overnight and that you, (like I did), might have those who will say that you couldn't possibly succeed. Comments like that virtually stopped when we became #7 and we had tremendous momentum.

Did I believe we could do it? I didn't have a doubt and I was willing to spend the time and the energy to make it happen.

Drive, will, determination, energy. Do you have the drive to win?

Do you have what it takes to fulfill your dream?

Do you have the will to win?

Do you have the determination to succeed?

Have you completed your written plan?

Do you have a firm timetable?

What is your first step?

You must be ready, if necessary for mid-course adjustments. When you have a clear goal about success and you have obstacles, which were not present when you designed your plan, you must evaluate whether or not you need to make a change.

Has the economy changed so dramatically that you could not make your goal?

What are your next steps if you have to make an adjustment in your plan?

Has the effort cost more than you budgeted? Has a key member of the team left the project or died? Have you thought about contingency plans? Always anticipate what might happen. Always remember that things can and do go wrong, so you have to be prepared to change course. Don't change too quickly. Don't change until you have carefully reviewed all of the options and determined that you cannot go forward as you had originally planned because of these dramatic changes.

Take some quiet planning and thinking time. Review the options with someone who has your goals and best interests in mind.

Even with changes, you can still succeed. It just might take a little longer and might have a different flavor.

Even with an adjusted plan, you will still need determination, drive and the will to succeed.

Exodus 5:18
Go therefore now, and work, for there shall no straw be given you, yet shall ye deliver the tale of bricks.

Deuteronomy 32:4
He is the Rock; his work is perfect; for all his ways are judgement. A God of truth and without iniquity, just and right is He.

Psalm 112:3
Wealth and riches shall be in his house; and His righteousness endureth forever.

> "The man who removes a mountain begins by carrying away small stones."
> William Faulkner

> "The ambitious will always be first in the crowd, he presseth forward, he looketh not behind him."
> Anonymous

> "Imagination is more important than knowledge. Knowledge is limited. Imagination encircles the world."
> Albert Einstein

"The world is moving so fast now-a-days that the man (or the woman) says it can't be done is generally interrupted by someone doing it.
Elbert Hubbard

"The secret of getting ahead is getting started. The secret of getting started is breaking your complex or overwhelming tasks into small manageable tasks and starting with the first one."
Mark Twain

"No one could tell me where my soul might be;
I searched for God and he eluded me;
I sought my brother out, and found all three."
Ernest Crosby

"I will tunnel a way."
Author Unknown

A prayer for the New Year and a new beginning:
"A Prayer for the New Year"
O year that is going, take with you
Some evil that dwells in my heart
Let selfishness, doubt,
With the old year go out --
With joy I would see them depart.

O year that is going, take with you
Impatience and willfulness -- and pride
The sharp word that slips
From those too hasty lips,
I would cast, with the old year aside.

O year that is coming, bring with you
Some virtue of which I have need;
More patience to bear
And more kindness to share
And more love that is true love indeed.
                    Laura F. Armitage

Notes:

Chapter 13

LEARN HOW TO SPEAK WELL AND BE A GREAT LISTENER

Most people have a favorite speaker or two. Someone you can listen to over and over again, even if they are saying the same thing. There is something about their voice or their tone or the rhythm of their delivery that is interesting.

Some have mastered the volume and pitch and you find yourself watching and waiting for the next phrase. You can hear a pin drop. You are on the edge of your seat.

Most people dream about delivering a speech like that. A message filled with power and force. A speech that will be remembered for weeks and even years. A speech that moved you to act or to think differently or even to tears. A speech that has you asking if, "the speech is available on video" so that you could play it over and over again.

You think about the crowd and the collective laughs and the collective silence. You watch the heads nodding and the bodies swaying and the reaction is almost universal. You can confirm that you are listening to a great orator.

A great speech can indeed be a powerful tool to convey a message, ask for action, and stop an action, to call for a vote or to stop a vote and - in my instance -- to ask for money.

The powerful orators of our day have had the benefit of television, but there isn't anything like seeing a seasoned orator live with a large audience. Most magnificent speakers seem to rise to the occasion and are even better when the stakes are higher and they are speaking before a large crowd.

I believe that great orators have received a gift from God, however, I also believe that you can train yourself to be a better speaker. If your plan is to speak in front of 50,000, then you must begin with a smaller group and hone your skills. You must be comfortable with the audience and with yourself and, if you believe it, and train for it, you can do it.

Many people report that giving a speech is their number one fear. Some report stomach aches, hives, shortness of breath and cold sweats before they have to make a speech. Some will use any excuse not to have to speak in front of a crowd and still many others simply refuse to speak, volunteering instead to take on other tasks.

After speaking for years in front of church groups, social and civic organizations and for college commencements, the size of the crowd has not been something to give me pause. I do want to make sure, however, that the things I can control have been attended to so that my speech is as much fun for me as it is for the audience.

I recently had a great opportunity. In the fall of 2002, I was asked to join the speaking tour for Bishop T. D. Jakes who has appeared on the cover of Time Magazine and who Time described as "America's greatest preacher." Pretty exciting.

This wonderful invitation is a great demonstration of so much of what is in this book. I felt I was ready to take on this challenge. I have reminded you to be ready for "new opportunities" and this was certainly an unbelievable one.

The Bishop had an idea to travel around the country with a program called, "God's Leading Ladies." The concept was not too complicated, but brilliant. The program would focus on women who wanted to "move to the next level" at home, in business, at their place of employment and in their lives. The speakers, all seasoned speakers, would focus on the things that many women missed along the way. Most had not had mentors or coaches and didn't have a chance to learn many of the things that are vital to succeeding.

The components stress personal relationships, particularly for the successful woman and how she must focus on her relationship at home. Other segments feature advice on financial stability and, particularly for women, how to plan for your retirement and the best instruments for investments at various stages of your life, as well as taking care of the mind, the body and the spirit.

I was asked to speak about leadership and I stress some characteristics, which are primary factors in the success of many people, and how the "little things" that can make a huge difference in whether or not you succeed. There is also a message for all the single women in the audience and a play presented in three acts which is part of the continuing theme about how to improve yourself. One of the highlights of the conference is a chance to hear how planning and the will to win are key elements in success and it is a wonderful, personal testimony from the Bishop. The one and a half day session closes with a challenge to "birth your dreams" and how you must prepare yourself for success. The early schedule took us to Jacksonville, Florida; Philadelphia and Charlotte. We returned to Philadelphia for a second session since the first sold out so quickly.

Tremendous crowds with a combined attendance of over 36,000. Our Master of Ceremonies, "Mr. Prime Time," Deion Sanders, a multi-talented athlete and most recently, a member of the award-winning Dallas Cowboys. He is now a CBS sports analyst and those who saw him as our Master of Ceremonies believe, as I do, that he was meant for this role.

Think about being on a program like this. Dream about it. Large groups. So, after audiences of several thousand in each city, it might seem a lot easier to get ready for a departmental meeting or a church group or a civic or neighborhood group and think about what you will say and how the message can be put into manageable pieces.

Remember that you must practice. Not to the point of memorizing the speech. This is always a dangerous thing since you might forget one word and then you are stymied.

Rather, take the speech challenge in little pieces. Don't make it too complicated. There are some basic principles, which will help you deliver an effective speech, and you can apply some of these steps when you have to make a presentation with a much smaller group.

1. Understand the purpose of the speech (sales, award presentation, general information, etc.)
2. Find out all you can about the audience. Are these experts in the field, friends of the award winner, etc?
3. Where will you be speaking? Know as much about the site as possible.
4. Know your subject matter.
5. Add humor to your remarks
6. Get a good night's rest
7. Make eye contact
8. Smile
9. Try not to read every word if you have notes or note cards
10. Make certain that you get your point/s across to the audience

I could add lots of other things to the list, such as voice control, movement on the stage, where to stand at the podium, differences in microphones (such as hand held, stationery, head mikes and lavalieres) are all commonly used, so I always recommend that a keynote speaker, or even one who is going to have a small part on the program, should arrive early enough to test the equipment. Most hotels have technicians to adjust the sound system and that is usually finished during the setting up of the room -- long before you and other program participants arrive.

Always wear comfortable clothes and shoes so they won't be a distraction. Don't chew gum. Also, have a glass of water handy.
In addition, don't apologize unless you make a serious mistake.

Don't start your remarks with "I wasn't really prepared" or other phrases that just take up time and do not win you any points with the audience.

Avoid:

1. "Boy, she's a tough act to follow."

I've followed Presidents; sports figures, Secretary of State Colin Powell and some of the most prominent business leaders in America and those words have never crossed my lips. The audience heard what you heard and they know that the previous speaker was very good, however, you will and should always plan to be just as good or even better when you deliver your speech.

2. "I'm really not prepared."

Those in the audience will immediately be disappointed and there isn't any reason for you to say this, but time and time gain, we hear this phrase by the novice speaker. Even if you are asked on the spot to say a few words, your response should be "I'll be happy to" and then proceed with some brief appropriate remarks about the occasion, the anniversary, the award or whatever the topic or purpose of the evening might be.

3. "I just found out about this yesterday."

This response shines a very unfavorable light on the host or the evening's organizers. Perhaps they had a speaker cancel at the last minute, perhaps someone is ill or they needed another speaker on the program. Whatever the reason, once you accept you should do all you can to deliver the best possible remarks, and never make excuses.

4. "I'm really nervous, so please bear with me."

Don't call attention to your anxieties. At a time like this, a little humor is called for in a speech. Your humorous opening will settle you down, get the audience to connect and give you an opportunity to have some additional time getting a feel for the room, the podium and your place on stage.

Get ready. Write several small speeches and deliver them at home to family and friends. Volunteer to participate in programs at church, with your book club, your social or civic groups or neighborhood associations.

You can also join Toastmasters, the premiere group for providing regular opportunities for novices and veterans alike to speak before different audiences.

You can contact Toastmasters by calling:

1-800-993-7732 or 1-949-858-8255

As you begin to speak in front of larger groups, ask a friend to come with you so that you have a trusted advisor to give you feedback. The audience might give you a standing ovation; however, you want to watch little habits that can, over time, turn into major distractions.

Watch your phrasing! Many have succumbed to filling in a silent moment with the same phrase over and over again. Careful listeners will hear, "um" "and" and "you know" over and over from some speakers. Also, some confuse "ask" with "ax" and aren't even aware of these things creeping into their language. Others drop their voice and you cannot hear them or their voice trails off at the end of every sentence.

Ask your friend to critique your stage presence. Do you appear comfortable? Was your hair, clothes, jewelry or makeup a distraction?

Was your voice loud enough? Did you sound timid or confident? Do you drop the volume of your voice at the end of the sentence? Is your delivery hesitant or forceful?

Also, points to consider:

1. Did you appear to know the material?
2. What was the reaction from the audience?
3. How was the timing of the speech - too long/too short?
4. Did you make eye contact?
5. Did you have to read your entire speech?
6. Did you connect your speech to the occasion?
7. Was your joke funny?
8. How was your overall delivery?
9. Did you seem to have stage presence?
10. Was your hair (or clothes, jewelry, makeup) a distraction?
11. Was your voice timid or forceful?
12. Could people in the back of the room hear you?
13. Are there any phrases you are repeating too much?
14. How was your closing?
15. Are people likely to remember any of the points you made?

There are, of course, a lot of other fine points to delivering great speeches, but if you start with this list, you will find that you will be able to take little steps to adjust your presentations and speeches. One of the most important things I can share is to have fun. The audience really wants you to succeed and you must always start with that thought.

Make sure that you take as much time as possible to prepare and confirm the one or two points you want to make.

What is the message you want to leave with the audience? Confirm that message and work on a speech that will help you deliver that message.

Are you comfortable giving a speech?

Why?

If you are not comfortable, why not?

What can you do to make giving speeches easier for you?

Who can help?

Suppose you are not in a work environment that requires you to give speeches, yet this is one of your goals. What can you do to put yourself in more places to give speeches?

How will you make this happen?

Do you have a hobby?

Write a brief speech about that and practice with a friend.

There are some other things that a leader needs to focus on in addition to being able to convey plans, goals and progress. A leader must also be a great listener. While people want to hear from the person in charge, they also want to make certain that their thoughts and ideas are valued and will be considered. Great listeners project their openness and accessibility.

Be a great talker and a great listener as well.

Are you a great listener?

How do you know that you are an attentive listener?

Have you ever started talking before the other person has finished talking?

Do you often ask questions?

Are you usually saying more than anyone else at a meeting?

Make sure to be sensitive about how much and how often you talk and whether or not you are giving others enough of an opportunity to voice their opinions and ideas.

Why is it important to be a great listener?

How can I become a better listener?

I Timothy 1:14
And the grace of our Lord was exceeding abundant with faith and love which is in Christ Jesus.

> "Laughter is the sun that drives winter from the human face."
> Victor Hugo

> "It takes three weeks to prepare a good ad-lib speech."
> Mark Twain

> "You will never will be the person you can be if pressure, tension, and discipline are taken out of your life."
> James G. Bilkey

> "You can't hold a man down without staying down with him."
> Booker T. Washington

> "The only place where success comes before work is in the dictionary."
> Vidal Sasson

"Act as if what you do makes a difference. It does."
William James

"I used to want the words, 'She tried' on my tombstone. Now I want 'She did it' on my tombstone."
Katherine Dunham

"In your lifetime, if you can come up with one original idea, you have accomplished a great deal."
Max Roach

Chapter 14

LEARN HOW TO PREPARE A GREAT MEETING AGENDA -
PRACTICE ORGANIZING A SUCCESSFUL MEETING

Some say it's the room, still others insist it is the shape of the table, but I know that one of the most critical elements of any meeting is the meeting agenda.

Start with the question, "what do you want to accomplish?" Make sure that others think that the topic is worth their time and that the meeting will accomplish your goal or at least set the course to accomplish the goal.

Some meetings are designed to just brief people about what has happened or what is going to happen. These briefing meetings are usually designed to support the internal communications strategy and go a long way toward keeping all employees informed. There may or may not be a section on the agenda to have questions from the participants. Also, it depends on how much time it takes to convey the information.

Let's take an example of a new senior executive coming to visit and he would like to have a meeting around an announcement about the company's plans for the next year.

A very simple agenda might look like this:

COMPANY
DATE
TIME
PLACE
NAME OF PERSON PRESIDING
PURPOSE (OPTIONAL)

I	WELCOME AND INTRODUCTIONS
II	REVIEW OF THE AGENDA
III	PRESENTATION BY ------ (NAME OF GUEST)
IV	DISCUSSION
V	OTHER BUSINESS
VI	ADJOURNMENT

Many companies and organizations have standard formats for meeting agenda, so you need to verify what is the rule if you are new to the organization. So many people tell me that they have never been responsible for organizing a meeting so this simple outline might prove helpful. For the more seasoned managers, the following are some tips and reminders about confirming the agenda and running a meeting and other details you need to review for each and every meeting. Your precision will mean that you are much more likely to finish the task and accomplish your goals for the meeting than if you were not careful in the preparation period.

Don't forget to review:
1. Purpose of the meeting
2. Participants
3. Time and location (be precise) and, end time when possible
4. If participants need to bring any materials
5. If this is but one meeting in a series
6. If the meeting is at or near a meal time, whether or not a meal will be served (and if so, are participants asked to pay)
7. Who can be called for information or questions
8. Who is responsible for any minutes, if required
9. Will there be special guests (people not normally included)
10. Appropriate time on the agenda for each item
11. Confirmation about who will actually Chair the meeting
12. Whether any special equipment is needed
13. If special dress is required, give the details

14. Are any special arrangements needed to either getting the material duplicated and mailed or delivered to the meeting participants?
15. Verify room arrangements
16. Review the dynamics of decision making
17. If this is a formal meeting, who will be the Parliamentarian?
18. Review your role and make sure you have everything you need to chair a great meeting

If you are not the Chair, make certain that you have read the material related to the meeting and any notes from the prior meeting. Take time to formulate your questions and, if you need to, make notes on the exhibits so that you are prepared to participate.

Many people tell me that they have trouble participating in meetings. Still others, the majority of whom are women, tell me that they are often ignored and their opinions discounted in meetings. Since this has happened with such frequency, many people sit quietly in meetings and do not speak up at all.

Here are a few tips to get ready to participate:

1. Be prepared for the meeting.
2. Arrive early and sit at or near the head of the table (it is a lot easier to focus on what you are going to say and a lot easier to concentrate on the discussion if you do not have to keep twisting and turning to the left and the right). You can focus your attention in one direction when the Chair is speaking (normally from the head of the table).
3. Organize your thoughts before you speak.
4. Make certain you have everyone's attention.
5. Make your point clearly or ask a pertinent question and have a follow-up question ready if you do not get an answer that satisfies you.

6. You can build your credibility by making sure that your questions are relevant and you are not asking about something that has already been covered.

7. Highlight key items like the budget or the timing of a project, important elements that will give an indication about the scope and focus of any effort.

8. If someone is taking minutes, indicate that you hope that your comments are recorded because you believe that the issue you surfaced is a key issue, worthy of monitoring and hearing a progress report at the next meeting.

9. Bring some additional information that the group might not have read. Make sure it is relevant.

10. Also focus on what is needed to get a vote on each topic. Decision-making is different for each group and each agenda and you need to make certain that you understand your role in each instance and are viewed as a great meeting participant.

Do you feel comfortable in meetings? At work? At church? In social groups? What can you do to improve your participation in meetings? What can you do to make certain that your comments at meetings are appreciated and not ignored?

In far too many meetings, we have seen people who will try to capotalize on someone else's ideas. These "second" speakers use phrases like: "That's the point I was trying to make" or "Precisely my point..." or "I'll say it in a slightly different way, but I had the same idea," however, we all know it was NOT their idea. We all know people who constantly start their sentences this way and, in effect, they are trying to take credit for someone else's idea. They know it, you know it and I know it. Don't fall into this trap. Great ideas, particularly those which have been well thoughtout, warrant a brief note or e-mail, to the Chair or your Department Head, quickly outlining your thoughts prior to the meeting. This is a great way to "confirm" your idea if you have had someone take credit for your work. Also, depending on the history with certain people who get credit for the work of others, or the culture of your organization, send a copy of your comments to another colleague and also bring a copy of your note to the meeting. a little advance work can make a world of difference.

Who can help?

What specific actions can you take to better understand group dynamics and the process of decision making?

Do you need to read additional material about decision-making techniques?

The Internet is a great resource. Start with a search of Women's Leadership. Also, review research reports at your local library. You can also check the colleges in your area. Many colleges have special Leadership Institutes for Women. Just like your Bible Study group at church, you can also start a Leadership Group for the Women in your community. Dream. Research. Act.

What can you do to do a better job getting ready for every meeting?

How can you run a better meeting?

Exodus 33:17
And the Lord said into Moses, I will do this thing also that thou hast spoken; for thou hast found grace in my sight and I know thee by name.

I Timothy 5:17 Pray without ceasing.

Genesis: 17:7
And I will establish my covenant between me and thee and thy seed

after thee in their generations for an everlasting covenant, to be a God unto thee, and to thy seed after thee.

John 1:16
And of his fullness have all we received, and grace for grace.

"You have to know you can win. You have to think you can win. You have to feel you can win.
Sugar Ray Leonard

"We can do no great things, only small things with great love."
Mother Teresa

"Never let your head hang down. Never give up and sit down and grieve. Find another way. And don't pray when it rains if you don't pray when the sun shines.
Satchel Paige

Chapter 15

TAKE CARE OF THE PEOPLE WHO WORK WITH YOU AND
FOR YOU

Make sure that you have a plan to provide staff training and
development opportunities. If you are the owner, the executive in
charge or the associate, make sure that you understand that
employees need and value training and the chance to attend
seminars and workshops to learn new skills.

Your support of these things will mean that employees will know
that you value them and want them to succeed. Many employee
satisfaction surveys confirm that people want additional money and
better retirement options, however, they often also cite the need for
additional training.

With increased capacities for computers and other systems, it is
important that employees feel that they have had the opportunity to
get the most from their equipment. Most employees know that
their knowledge is transferable and, while they might not be
looking for another place to work, you too will benefit from their
increased knowledge.

In an earlier chapter, we reviewed saying thank you to employees.
Make sure that you find appropriate ways to cite and reward. Do
what you can within your budget limitations and, when possible, do
this on a regular basis. Say "thank you" often.

You need to exhibit the sensitivity and understanding about the
different racial and ethnic groups and religious preferences as well.
Other employees will note your examples.

Each employee is special and you need to make certain that each
one is treated with dignity and respect.

What have I done to support employees?

What is the most important thing that my employees need?

For those who are not supervisors or owners, have you identified the top three things you would like to do to strengthen your skills:

I often describe diversity in many ways; however, I like to always remind people that it also means that we understand that we can learn something from people who have different backgrounds.

How do you describe diversity?

What have you done to help foster understanding in your work environment?

Genesis: 7:1
And the Lord said unto Noah, Come thou and all thy house into the ark; for thee have I seen righteous before me in this generation.

Exodus 4:12
Now therefore go, and I will be with thy mouth, and teach thee what thou shalt say.

> "Do not waste a minute -- not a second -- in trying to demonstrate to others the merits of your performance. If your work does not vindicate itself, you cannot vindicate it."
>
> Thomas Wentworth Higginson

"Say not always what you know, but always know what you say."

Claudius

"I have never been hurt by anything I didn't say."

Calvin Coolidge

"Life must be lived moment by moment. Each moment carries a message, a lesson for us."

Dr. David K. Reynolds

"The final test of a leader is that he leaves behind him in other men the conviction and the will to carry on. The genius of a good leader is to leave behind him a situation which common sense, without grace or genius, can deal with successfully.

Walter Lippmann

Notes:

Chapter 16

HAVE A FIRM HANDSHADE

A word about handshakes. Too many people shake with too firm a grip. A few years ago, I was going through a receiving line and after shaking hands with one individual, I felt a severe pain in my hand and knew that it had been injured. I had to rest it for several weeks, wore an elastic guard and had difficulty signing letters with my usual flourish. A firm grip, please, but not too firm.

Again, practice, practice, practice and ask a friend for a reaction.

How is my handshake?

Do I make eye contact when I shake someone's hand?

Who can help?

Deuteronomy 18:13
Thou shalt be perfect with the Lord thy God.

2 Samuel 22:33
God is my strength and power and he maketh my way perfect.

> "I will smile at friend and foe alike and make every effort to find, in him or her, a quality to praise, now that I realize the deepest yearning of human nature is the craving to be appreciated."
>
> Anonymous

"Tell a person they are brave and you help them become so."

Thomas Carlyle

"The potential of the average person is like a huge ocean unsailed, a new continent unexplored, a world of possibilities waiting to be released and channeled toward some great good."

Brian Tracy

Chapter 17

READ, READ, READ

Keep up with current events and know what is going on in your company. How do community, national or international events effect you? What are the implications of the news?

Find a way to expand your mind. Find out about something new. If you like flowers learn the names of new flowers, if you want to improve a certain business skill, read about the new techniques. Every year, a large number of new business, relationship, technical, sales and marketing books are published, so you will not have any trouble finding out about any area you wish to explore.

Keeping up to date about current events will make conversations at work much easier. You will know about the latest political, economic, social and neighborhood issues. If crime is a major issue in your area, if effects you. If interest rates change, you need to be aware of the change. If a national or international leader is visiting your city, you need to know the details and if there is a new development or invention related to your business or company, it would be smart to know about this report as well.

You need to keep up to date for several reasons, the least of which is that you will be much more interesting. Your participation in company and personal conversations will be livelier and you will find that, if you focus on a few things and are known as someone who is knowledgeable in those areas, you will be the person who is called upon to respond to questions in your area.

You cannot guarantee that you will be the center of attention, but you will be a more comfortable and confident communicator.

This push for you to read will have another benefit. You will no doubt want to further investigate certain things so you will go to different parts of your city and state, or visit other companies and note the resources in local libraries or go to the library in a neighboring town.

Read, read, and read.   Know what's going on in your world.

What do you normally read?

What would you like to learn more about?

What will you do to make that happen?

Who can help?

What do you want to focus on in your new learnings?

Why?

Are you an expert in a certain field?

If so, how do you keep up to date?

If not, do you want to become an expert in a certain area?

How will you accomplish this?

Are there specialty/expert areas at your place of employment?

Do you know what they are and the qualifications of these positions?

What does reading do to help you? What are some of the new things you wish to read?

Will you make time each week to go to the library?

Psalm 35:28
And my tongue shall speak of thy righteousness and of thy praise all the daylong.

Genesis 11:1
And the whole earth was of one language, and of one speech.

Exodus 35:31
And he hath filled him with the spirit of God, in wisdom, in understanding, and in knowledge, and in all manner of workmanship.

Proverbs 1:28-30

Then shall they call upon me, but I will not answer; they shall seek me early, But they shall not find me. For that they hated knowledge, and did not choose the fear of the Lord, They would none of my counsel; they despised all my reproof.

"The best of all things is to learn. Money can be lost or stolen, health and strength may fail, but what you have committed to your mind is yours forever."

Louis L'Amour

"Be well trained and willing to be re-trained and make a commitment to be a life-long learner."

Marian L. Heard

"We cannot become what we need to be, remaining what we are."

Max Dupree

"You can chain me, you can torture me, you can even destroy this body, but you will never imprison my mind."

Mahatma Gandhi

"Read, every day, something no one else is reading. Think every day, something no one else is thinking. Do, every day, something no one else would be silly enough to do. It is bad for the mind to be always of unanimity"

Christopher Morley

"Whatever you can do, or dream you can - begin it. Boldness has genius, power, and magic in it."

Goethe

"Even if you are on the right track, you'll get run over if you just sit there."

Will Rogers

"Each step should give you a base for a prudent next step so that you can move steadily toward a new role without ever contemplating a move that presents an unwarranted risk to what you have already built."

Robert K. Greenleaf

"For you know the plans you have for me, Lord. Plans to prosper me and not to harm me, plans to give me a hope and a future."

Beth Moore

Notes:

Chapter 18

LEARN ABOUT SPORTS.

SPORTS ARE THE CONVERSATION OF MEN.

GET IN THE CONVERSATION.

GET IN THE GAME.

Make it a point to read about sports. You can start the day with the business page, then the sports page and next the front-page. Find out who is playing what.

I am the wife of a sports fan and the mother of two sons who are sports fans. I learned when our sons were around six years old and started playing organized sports in a serious way that sports would play a big part in our lives and they still do.

In business and industry, particularly at the top there are many more men than there are women and I have found that men tend to follow sports. At the dinner table at my house, our young sons would focus on the sport of the season and we would move from football to soccer and next on to basketball (both the NBA and particularly, college basketball) and then baseball. We'd discuss the Super Bowl, the World Series, the standings and the rankings as well as other national tournaments and, of course, the Final Four.

In order to do what I am advising you to do, I had to focus on sports. It was not a natural inclination, however, I am certainly glad that I not only developed an interest in the various games, but found that the lives of the players, the standings, the outstanding accomplishments and the championship games provide lots of excitement and form the basis for over 75% of the conversations with men. The discussions are wide ranging-from the NCAA Final Four to the World Series to the antics of certain players on and off the court or the field, to coverage of any local decisions about coaches and managers to the cost of tickets to the actual game. There is a lot of attention paid to the Super Bowl, men's and women's tennis and, since the dramatic and unparalleled play of Tiger Woods, more and more about golf.

My husband and I took golf lessons a few years ago and now he plays regularly. I play less frequently because of the time it takes, however, I do enjoy the lovely golf courses and the time spent with either my husband or other good friends. Even though I don't play regularly, I know that it is important to keep up to date about the major tournaments, the leading players in the world and information about some of the courses we have played.

These sports-related conversations are always fun. Sometime there are friendly bets (all very legal, of course) on the outcome of the game. In addition, particularly when there is a rivalry such as that between the New York Yankees and the Boston Red Sox, the conversation about each of the games becomes very interesting and very exciting.

Every time these two teams play against each other throughout Boston and in New York, there is a feeling of anticipation about the outcome days before the game and then the details of the game are reviewed and discussed after the game -- over and over again. We have been lucky enough to be in the stadium when these two great teams have played and you can be sure that there is a lot more enjoyment when you can discuss some of the recent events on the field, the status of an injured player or any other things which have been the headline on the sports page!

There are great pitching rivalries and close attention is paid to the decision of each manager about when they change pitchers. The decisions, of course are talked about for days, depending on which one actually made the right call about when to "bring in the lefty."

No matter what sport, think about all of the things that you can discuss and the ways for you to "get in the conversation." The condition of the fields, the weather, the calls by the umpires or the referees, decisions by the respective commissioner about new rules (strike zone in baseball) and overtime issues in football are debated in heated tones. When the vote is counted about who is going into any "Hall of Fame," there is another discussion. Every single trade and the draft picks given up to get a certain player are rehashed again and again and if you are not aware of any of this, you are not going to be able to "get in the conversation."

Yes, men do talk about other things and so do women, however, I encourage you to have at least a working knowledge about the major sports issues of the day and, in particular, when these issues make headlines. What are some of the other topics? It would be helpful to be versed about the economy, politics (both local and national), interest rates, major crime stories and the impact of the weather on business. Still others might focus on the best-selling book list and regale you with the accounts of his or her favorite author's latest novel.

Many men in business also talk about elected officials, major construction projects, their families, international issues such as the war in Iraq or disturbances in the Middle East and Africa. They might also focus on important community events since most major companies sponsor key award and fund raising dinners. In other words, current events! Read, read, and read so that you are up to date about a variety of issues and topics.

However, if you work with a majority of men, like I have done for decades, before most meetings begin, during lunches and dinners and in small groups, the conversation inevitably will turn to sports. It is the language of men. I encourage everyone, particularly women who are in business at any level to keep up to date with sports. There are news stories about the cost of every new stadium and its impact on ticket prices, the traffic patterns or the support of public transportation and the case -- or lack thereof -- in getting to the parks. There are stories about the millions of dollars paid to the latest superstar. Then, there are stories about who is on the disabled list and "is questionable" in terms of whether or not he or she will play the next big game.

There are discussions about the coaches, the food, the parking and the game itself, particularly if a team is in the playoffs or is close to getting there.

The discussion is also about the "bad behavior" of some of the players. If it's in the headlines, it will be discussed just before the "next meeting" and if someone else doesn't bring up the headlines about the incident, I will, just to get the conversation started.

Some men and some women will never have an interest in sports and that is perfectly acceptable, however, the next time that you are in a group or in your own family setting and the conversation turns to sports, you might want to re-think your position if you have not been able to join in the discussion!

If you can't insert sports in the conversation or don't know enough to participate, then turn to current events. Recent news accounts about the accounting industry; illegal stock transactions and personal perks raise questions about corporate practices. You can talk about the local real estate market and the change in property values. You can discuss major events at your church, particularly if they involve large community groups. Most people enjoy discussing the movies. State your views and ask for a discussion. This will be a great way to let people know you are keeping up to date, reading and are able to discuss many different topics.

It's often the little things that will establish, confirm and maintain your working relationships and I know that sports have enhanced mine. I often have the opportunity to attend games and that, of course, means that I will have a personal opinion -- yes -- a personal opinion about the play on the field or the court.

If you are in an area where sports are not a major focus, find out what is the major focus. Is it politics? Is it local development issues? Is it the local economy? What is it? You need to know today and make certain that you keep current, because the focus at any given time of the year might change and you want to be able to be a part of major discussions.

Sports, however, in my world, mean that I not only get in the conversation, but also because I keep up to date, I will often be able to lead the conversation. Remember that it's the little things. Don't eliminate yourself. Find a way to connect and be able to discuss current events.

Do you keep up to date with the key issues in your company?
Or your field/business?

What are they?

What are the key issues in your community?

Do you feel you are knowledgeable enough to "get in the conversation?"

What are you doing to keep up to date?

What do you currently read?

What do you think you should add to your reading list?

Have you ever felt that you were excluded from "the conversation" because you were not up to date about the topic?

What was the topic?

Have you ever felt excluded because the topic was sports?

Do you plan to read the sports pages to "get in the conversation?"

What will be your first step?

Mark 11:22
And Jesus answering saith unto Him, Have faith in God.

1 Timothy 2:7
Consider what I say; And the Lord give thee understanding in all things.

I Chronicles 2:4
And my speech and my preaching (was) not with enticing words Of man's wisdom, but in demonstration of the Spirit and of power.

> "Our greatest glory consists not in never falling, but in rising every time we fall."
>
> Oliver Goldsmith

Chapter 19

THE PERSONAL SIDE OF LEADERSHIP - EXHIBIT
PATIENCE - NOURISH YOUR PERSONAL RELATIONSHIPS -
TAKE TIME TO ENJOY EACH DAY - REMEMBER THAT
GREAT ATTITUDE

The personal side of leadership is just that -- it's personal.

You have to be who you are and never forget that. Your
background, your family, your experiences all make up who you
are.

I'm going to encourage you to approach everything with a "can do"
spirit and an attitude that you "can win." I believe that most
people can enhance their capacity to become a happy, loving,
supportive and positive person and work hard to help others see that
side of them. I see the good in people, I see the joy on the face of
a child, I love the sun and I love the quiet of the rain. I don't like
bitterly cold weather, yet I appreciate the freshly fallen snow on the
trees and the sheer beauty of that sparkle when the sun hits the
limbs. I applaud others and know that God has truly blessed my
family and me. How would you describe yourself?

Are you patient? Have you ever taken time to explore the woods,
rocks, the beach and everything you see walking or exploring other
neighborhoods? Time, patience and examination. So it is with
business. Even great plans cannot be completed in a day or a week.
The best details need to be refined and re-cast more than a few
times, so patience is needed. Work at being patient with yourself
and others.

ATTITUDE

When someone asks me, "How I am doing?" my answer is always
the same; "I am FABULOUS, ABSOLUTELY FABULOUS." It
amazes and confounds people and now they expect that answer and

brighten up as they in turn answer me with a great adjective. Some will use magnificent, or wonderful or great. Others will tell me that they are fabulous as well. It is a feeling that is infectious, bringing smiles to faces and laughter all around.

People want to be around happy people. Critical people, people who will constantly question your every move, those who are not happy and complain about everything will "zap" your energy.

These are "emotional thieves" and you must protect yourself. Emotional thieves are those people who will take your time and your energy and you can feel yourself becoming impatient every time they begin to speak. They are stealing your energy. Don't let them do it. These people are sometimes unable to feel great or happy and, try as you might, most days they do not have anything positive to say. You cannot avoid them at all times, however, you would do well to spend as little time as possible since these people can only help themselves learn to appreciate life.

Do you have unhappy people in your life?

Who are they?

Make a pact with yourself that you don't want to spend too much time with them. This is important because you must -- must -- preserve your energy. You can feel yourself cringing when that individual is around -- you know that no matter which subjects surface, they will find a way to complain. They usually do not have great family or personal relationships and the main focus of their conversation is usually about themselves, their opinions or their possessions. The are quick to frown and enjoy laughing at the expense of others. They are usually not well read and so it is difficult to have a meaningful conversation with them. If you have these people in your life, try not to sit next to them in meetings.

Work at speaking to them but not getting involved in long conversations. I have found that others give them a wide circle as well, since most people have identified them as problems.

Remember that you don't want to have your energy dissipated by someone who is always unhappy.

How will you manage to control the time you spend with the "downers?"

Remember the next paragraphs and you will understand why it is important to protect your energy. You will need it for more important things and wasting it on people, who will not and, perhaps cannot be happy, will not help you achieve your goals.

A Heardism -- "Surround yourself with happy people."

Millions of people went to sleep last night. Some didn't wake up. Of those who woke up, some couldn't get up. Those who woke up and could get up, have a tremendous responsibility to do something wonderful with the day. You have woken up and gotten up, so do something wonderful today!

Remember, every day you wake up and can get up, you must do something significant.

You are a special person. Make sure that those you spend time with are going to support you, encourage you and, when appropriate give you helpful feedback and constructive criticism. Learn to ask for feedback. Be open to helpful suggestions, particularly from people you know only want the best for you.

Make time to enjoy each day and appreciate what you have. Yes, continue to dream, but don't let the focus of what you don't have obscure the wonder of what you already have. Appreciate the little things.

Take time for your spouse or significant other. My husband and I review the calendar every month and, even with my incredibly busy schedule, we make sure that we have crossed out days, some evenings and long week-ends to spend time together. We also make sure to plan vacations far enough in advance so that they are on the calendar and the tickets are purchased. Yes, I have had to change more than a few plans when major companies are trying to schedule meetings around the CEO's hectic schedule and have had to take important conference calls while away, but yet we are working very hard at protecting this time away and making it more of a priority and, quite frankly, we think we are much better at it now than we were a few years ago.

How are you doing spending time with loved ones?

We are so lucky and blessed. Our sons and daughters-in-law are wonderful and have given us four precious grandchildren. Jewels all and we make time to get together and we also arrange to be with each family. It does take planning, but it is so well worth the effort.

Do you take time for yourself?

Do you and your spouse and/or significant other spend enough time together?

What can you do to add more family/personal time to your schedule?

How can you make this time a priority?

This next section is a critical one. It is about personal friendships. If you can't make a list of great and good friends, then you have some serious catching up to do.

Friendships enrich our lives and yet I have met too many women who tell me that they have become too busy to maintain friendships. Some can't even remember when they have visited, dined or talked with someone for other than business purposes. Where is their joy? It is usually missing. Friendships mean laughter. They mean that there are people who care for you and people you care for as well. You have common interests and respect for each other. You are interested in their family and in their health as well as their success. It is a critical dimension of life and I encourage those of you who can't make a list to start right now making ways and finding ways to connect in a significant way with other women.

Many people say you need several different kinds of friends. You don't have to label them, but look at this list and see if you can put a name or two (or more) beside each category:

1. Someone you love to talk with
2. A person who will listen to you
3. Someone you can call at 3 a.m. if you feel like talking
4. A person who you would call when death or problems occur
5. Someone who will celebrate your successes or help you when you fail
6. Someone who calls you just to check on you
7. Someone you call to check on
8. Someone who is concerned about your health and happiness
9. Someone who loves to spend time with you and you with her/them

You can add to this list, however, the main purpose is that you have friends who really care about you.

I have, no question, worked at nurturing my friendships -- with calls, cards, letters, and visits. In turn, many others remember my birthday, call to see what is new in my world and the state of my energy. Still others call to schedule visits, talk about recent novels or movies or a problem about their marriage, health or finances.

Long time friends are a big part of my life's joy and bring a feeling of contentment.

They know all about you and still love you!

GOLDEN FRIENDSHIPS

This section is about my friendships from childhood. The majority is still in Connecticut and I am happy to say that we have found frequent occasions to visit and while I continue to add to this list with people from Boston and other parts of the country, however, this group forms the core.

If you can't make a list of great and good friends --- I will say it again -- you have some serious catching up to do. Start now to reach out to others.

There are a lot of definitions of friendship, but one of my favorites is "a true friend is one you can call at 3 o'clock in the morning." I have such friends. The list is rich and long and their names are in this book. Many are friends I have had since the 5th grade, a number of others I met in junior high school and still others in high school or when my husband and I started dating. Yes, that means that these are friends of 40 and 50 years.

What does it take to sustain a friendship? Are you willing to take the time to have a friend? Take the time to be a friend?

Are you a caller? Do you prefer to write a letter?

Do you have a friend you can call on when you have a problem?

Do friends call on you when they have a problem?

Do you enjoy spending time with your friends?

I am really blessed, because I have a number of friends who simply call or write to "check on me."

Friends come to visit just to see my artwork, visit my office and spend time with us at our home. We talk about children, family issues, trips, problems, health, diets and lots and lots of novels as well as current movies. Some call when they want to discuss retirement plans, decisions about getting a divorce, illness or family trauma. Yes, even with this busy schedule, I find time to listen and share and they do as well.

My friends check on my emotional health and we talk about what "rocks" we have been in our families and remind ourselves to "stop and visit and relax and play."

Some of my friends like Rita Hayes, Margaret "Pickles" MacIntosh and Beverly Lewis write and call. These friends call just to say hello and write to keep in touch. Rita and I often talk, even now, for extended periods and I visit when I travel to Connecticut and she, in turn, has come to visit me. When our children were younger, it was not uncommon for us talk for hours. Our favorite time was talking while we finished cleaning the kitchen after dinner. It was never boring!!!

When our children were young, my husband and I made our children a priority, never missing a PTA meeting, a "back-to-school night" or being at home to help with homework and making sure that our sons were with us for lots of family trips. Whenever we entertained, we always included "the family" so that other families could spend time with our children and their children as well.

Friendships were always important and each of us works very hard at keeping in touch.

Rita was the first friend to come to see my artwork and I was the first friend she turned to when she was reviewing her retirement options. She and others call to see if I am really ok since they know that our families have had several recent deaths and continue to struggle with some very serious illnesses in both of our families.

Pickles as she is affectionately known, calls and writes as well and we have been friends since our teen years. We visit and talk and exchange wonderful notes about what is happening in our worlds. She and her husband, Bobby, and my husband and I went out on our first date together.

Bobby had introduced us two weeks earlier and a double date seemed more than appropriate. Long-term friends. Yes. That introduction was over 43 years ago. Through laughter and tears, busy family schedules, major health issues and work schedules, we have always found time to be together. We have also spent time together as we travel to family reunions and for celebrations for the children. She keeps me informed about what is taking place in my old area of Connecticut and will leave a message about the illness of a mutual friend so that I can send a card and make a call. She keeps me up to date about church matters related to our former church and those who have moved or changed jobs. She has given me a rare gift of "connection."

Beverly Lewis has been a very good friend and also, like I do, understands the challenges of caring for elderly parents. We talk about the common points in our lives and we all work hard at keeping in touch. There are also friends who have supported me, like Suzy Long, Terry Thompson, Marlene George, Mary Mellow, Anna Mellow, Midgie Tavares, Martha Tavares and Hazel McNair. They were frequent guests at our home in Connecticut and as many have retired or celebrated special things related to their families, we have traveled back to Connecticut to make sure to participate in their special days. If I really had a problem, I know they would respond and they know I would as well, just as we have in the past.

My friend, Carol Ciraulo, a friend from the 5th grade checks on my emotional health. And we talk about the illnesses in our respective families and our plans for our next get-together. We find time to keep in touch --no matter what is going on in our lives. With spouses, we travel together and write and call and now we even e-mail. We remind ourselves to "stop and visit and relax and play" and plan our time together at least a year in advance.

Even though we have lived a coast away from each other since we graduated from high school, and she has lived as far away as Hawaii, this distance has not dulled our friendship. She refers to me as her best friend and we are the oldest friends to each other. She and her husband recently built a new house and, imagine they have built a room for my husband and me to remind us to visit often. We recently visited with them and I must tell you that my room is beautiful. It is the blue room! We have encouraged each other and from our days in high school, been great competitors and helped each other. I know that if I were to ask, she would do anything to help and she knows this is true of me as well. She and her husband, Joe, continue to be great friends. Do you have people like this in your life?

My friend, Jane Zanardi and I met at the University of Bridgeport and since 1963, she and I have written two and often three times a week since that time and still continue to write. Can you imagine 30 years of letters?

I know it's hard to believe, but we write real letters every single week.

Not e-mails, but real letters on beautiful cards and on lovely stationery. I frequently look in stationery stores just to find beautiful paper to write to Jane. Her husband, Peter and my husband, Winlow, have become good friends and the four of us meet half way for dinners and visits and just to keep in touch. She started "stamping" a few years ago and every time I travel, I try to find her an unusual stamp. She makes beautiful cards and magnets as well and they are real treasures. Such a talented friend. I tell her that I know she has offered to make some more note cards and magnets for me, but I am very careful about who gets her beautiful handiwork.

Our letters are rich with the stories of the engagements, the weddings, the children and the deaths of parents, the tears of our children, the family divorces, the moves, the health issues, the decisions related to our children, our spouses and our own. We also write about the work challenges and our hobbies. She sings and volunteers at animal shelters in addition to stamping. I am painting and writing so we both lead full and active lives yet we find time to keep in touch. She recently took piano lessons and I took swimming lessons and, in our letters, we keep each other up to date about our successes and failures. We have shared the stories about spouses and our various trips and the stories about her pets and our jokes about pets, since we haven't had any in over a decade. We are both walkers and try to faithfully report on our habits.

We have laughed and cried about the illnesses and deaths in our families as well as how we have watched as our young children were hurt or disappointed and sometimes made what we consider to be horrible decisions. Through it all, we always make time to keep in touch with what many people say is "a lost art" and that is by writing letters.

Can you imagine the letters between friends that have now spanned over 30 years? If I have one regret is that we both didn't save all the letters and yet we often reflect on the paths our lives have taken in the past decades and know that we can depend on each other. A little bit of humor -- we believe that we have avoided therapy because we have written everything in our letters and given each other great advice -- and it was free!

A bit about my beloved SSL's. This is the great ladies club from high school and, since 1955, as a group, we have been friends. Some met before the first grade, others in grammar or junior high, but we formed a group in high school and have been a part of this group ever since then.

What does SSL stand for? Smart, strong ladies!!!

Their names, too, are listed in this book and every few weeks or so, there is a pot luck dinner in Connecticut and they are wonderful about checking my schedule so that I can attend. The laughter starts as soon as the car hits the driveway of the hostess and lasts until three people start yawning, or our sides are too sore to laugh any longer.

We have traveled together --just the girls -- to California and Las Vegas and had wonderful lunches and dinners at well-known restaurants in Massachusetts and Connecticut. (We invite the spouses twice a year to our dinners, so our husbands know each other as well.)

This year, they spent a weekend in Boston and I had the pleasure of showing them my great city. The tours and walks were wonderful, however, the best part of the visit was the time spent laughing and sharing our problems as well as our plans for the future. We even confirmed our next two sites - San Francisco in 2004 and Orlando in 2005 and, in each case, like I served as the hostess for Boston, the hostesses are hard at work confirming plans for us to get together. I know that we will also schedule a trip to New York as well. Do you have friends like this?

Each of us has shared our hopes and dreams. We have supported each other through the death of many parents (and, as a group, they came to the recent funeral of my father). We have buried siblings, spouses and a child and have cried together when our own members have died. We have all baked, hosted what can only be thousands of Tupperware, Coppercraft Guild and Princess House parties

We have also made gallons of clam and onion dip and baked ten thousand batches of brownies for the various club meetings and dinners. Each of us has hosted and planned and, as Kathy Clark says, "we have remained friends and avoided any problems because we are a group of equals." We are teachers, administrators, nurses, secretaries, managers, para-legals and business owners and yet we all feel that we can comfortably welcome each other into our homes and, for decades, welcome each other into our lives.

Thank you Rosemary Lankton, Eve Smith, Judy Solo, Nancy Murray, Evelyn Thayer, Carolyn Martin, Kathy Clark, Carol Ciraulo, Ann Roviello, Mary Sandburg, Annette Cullen, Judy Curran, Frannie Wadeka, Joan Gallos and the late Carolyn Thorne. Also, Natalie Siavrakas who was my study partner and in 1961 called me, just like you would call someone to go the movies or I would call her to go shopping or to New York and she said, "Let's go to college." And we did and, Nats, thanks again for the call.

Who are your friends?

Who would call you a friend?

What will you do to enhance your friendships?

As I write this book, it is the year of our 40th anniversary and my husband and I are planning lots of time together with our children and grandchildren. My husband, Winlow, is the real star in my world, and we spend time going to church, visiting with friends, being together at home just reading and now playing a little golf.

I also call my sisters Patricia, Phyllis and Gail great friends as well. Every few weeks, we schedule a luncheon together to visit and get caught up and, over the years, we have supported the special occasions for each child and celebrated with our parents the many holiday dinners and, as in the case over the years, "a dinner just to see each other."

Family and friends -- a great investment!!!

We like to celebrate and encourage you to plan and have lots of gatherings. Your life with be enriched by these times and, I guarantee, will be of great comfort in times of stress and when problems surface in other areas of your life. Life isn't just about work. It is also about relationships.

How do you celebrate with your family?

Do you make it a priority?

What can you do to nurture your friendships?

Notes:

Chapter 20

WATCH AND LEARN. GREAT LEADERS SET GREAT EXAMPLES.

A few words here about the other great leaders, friends, mentors and supporters. We all have them in our lives and it is worth taking time to acknowledge them. Ray Chambers and his dear wife, Patti. My life has changed since I met Ray. We have worked together on such diverse things as organizing the Points of Light Foundation for President Bush (#41) to America's Summit with all living Presidents and Colin Powell.

Ray, along with Geoff Boisi, organized a wonderful national organization called, Mentor, the National Mentoring Partnership. Talk about leadership, these two Co-founders, along with the National Executive, Gail Manza spearhead efforts to make certain that every child who needs one can have a Mentor. Ambitious? Absolutely! Needed? Definitely.

Have we met the goal yet? No. Are we moving in the right direction? I will add a resounding yes!

Gail's gift is that she is research oriented, so she has carefully laid out the case for the need for additional caring adults. Geoff and Ray have not only helped confirm the plans and this critical case for support, but have been personally involved in recruiting a terrific Board of Directors and Co-Chairing this vital agency.

At the Points of Light Foundation, where President Bush still serves as the Honorary Chairman, our staff leader, Bob Goodwin has served as the President and Chief Executive Officer and has led with great distinction. He is a master at planning and charting the course of our organization and has been named to the list of the 50 top national non-profit leaders in America.

Ray and I have worked on these Boards and issues and other efforts all designed to support the children and youth of America and I know when he is involved that it is very special.

Be open to new opportunities. I know when Ray calls; it is surely to be a great adventure "on the way to helping others." He is truly one of America's great and good volunteers.

Also, note the United Way Board list -- dedicated volunteers and true believers. A special note about those who have served in the key role of Board Chairman. Thank you, Bink Garrison, Bill van Faasen, Leo Breitman, Tom O'Donnell (who has served for three terms and has a special place on my speed dial) Ben Taylor and David Spina. Each one has brought insightful thinking and made a special contribution to our incredible organization.

You can read the papers and find out what NOT to do and the recent reports about Enron, World Com and Tyco tell about how some leaders get off track, however, you can also learn great lessons by watching those who run multi-billion dollar companies and small organizations, as well if you will just focus and learn. Let me tell you about the lessons from all of my corporate Board leaders.

Each exhibits a style and skill set worth emulating.

Each leader has connected to the community and supports not only the United Way, but many other great educational, youth and neighborhood development causes such as affordable housing and job training.

Each has a keen sense of humor and doesn't take life too seriously. They have fun "at the office" and after meetings as well. Each plans an annual strategy session that dissects the current and future challenges and opportunities. These retreats and strategy sessions are well planned and, in some instances, well-known experts are brought in to lead a discussion about critical issues facing the company. They all also start with the basic - A WRITTEN PLAN! So much of what I have written here I have seen put into place at these companies. This is not something I have read about, but something I have participated in, so when you look at any of the lists in this book, know that those leading great companies have checked off all the boxes and more!

Each has been a champion in terms of supporting women and people of color and certainly this author. Talk about networking, they could teach an advanced course. Each is competitive and wants to succeed. Each has determination, drive and the will to win. Each believes in "customer service." Each is a great listener and knows the value of surrounding himself with good people. They have all had top positions for years and yet are still exhibiting determination and energy.

Each has had adversity related to the economy, acquisitions, world events and personnel issues, yet their leadership skills have paved the way to a systematic review, decisions and then action.

Plus, they are all really nice people and they have been generous and responded with support and time whenever I have asked. They also all love sports, particularly baseball, football and golf, and each has a wife who has been a real partner, so this is one group who talks "runs, touchdowns and eagles" as well.

As you might have read on the back cover, and in the interest of full disclosure, I have served for a number of years on both the non-profit and corporate Boards I have cited. Monthly meetings and United Way work have given me numerous opportunities to observe how each group functions and the contributions being made by the respective leader.

I have also served, and continue to serve on several other Boards, and they are all great organizations: Dana Farber Cancer Institute, Fairfield University, the New England Aquarium, Berea College and Family Support America. Each has a mission I believe in and a great leadership team, an involved Board and is making great contributions in their respective communities.

In this book, I have focused on the Points of Light Foundation, Mentor and corporate Boards cited here as a response to the questions on notes, e-mails and evaluations from several major speeches and workshops and, in particular, questions from the "God's Leading Ladies" Conferences. The majority of people asked about corporate Boards, volunteering through the Points of Light Foundation and the United Way and becoming a Mentor or securing a Mentor for their children or themselves.

WHO ARE THE PEOPLE WHO LEAD THESE GIANT COMPANIES?

For now, concentrate on some of what you have already read in this book and look for the elements of leadership which are most important to you, as you review where you are in your career.

Meet my corporate leaders:

FLEETBOSTON FINANCIAL
Chad Gifford and Terry Murray from FleetBoston Financial (Much of the success of our personnel administration area is due to one of the human resource giants in America, Anne Sczostak, the EVP and Corporate Director of Human Resources and Diversity.) They know "the real art of the deal" and can give a primer not on Negotiating Skills 101, but the advanced courses. The history of multiple acquisitions tell you that this team knows about a win-win philosophy. They believe that good people should be supported and they give employees the opportunity to move within the company and have different experiences in the company. It's experience money can't buy and a solid plan to develop Fleet's people. They also have great vision-where are we going?

The company prides itself in terms of community response and supports a very long list of issues and agencies including education, children, job training and affordable housing. They have carefully reviewed "next steps" in terms of future opportunities as well as strategies to progress during a tough economy. I've watch and learned.

Fleet has focused on services in poor areas and their strategy reflects their belief that banking services should be avail able in every neighborhood. They have consistently worked on a plan to make sure that low to moderate-income families have a chance to own a home, get a loan and participate as full citizens. They have underwritten more than a few projects to support this plan.

BLUE CROSS AND BLUE SHIELD

Bill Van Faasen from Blue Cross and Blue Shield of Massachusetts. I will also add Joe Patnchak, the SVP of Human Resources (and, before him, Art Banks) who is responsible for the flow and implementation of staff support and training. Bill is a giant in the field of organizational development. He has great insight about how to tap talent and challenge his executive staff and thousands of associates as well.

Bill has led by example, supporting major community groups in leadership roles. Bill also wants to make sure that health care is as affordable as possible and leads in the research and discussion on this issue.

He has led his company through very serious economic and business challenges and has put plans in place, not only for future growth, but sustainability as well. He supports personal and professional development and makes certain that his Executive Staff and a number of associates participate in community leadership roles.

LIBERTY MUTUAL GROUP

Ted Kelly and Gary Countryman from Liberty Mutual Group. Helen Sayles, the SVP and Manager of Human Resources and Administration lead much of the design and implementation for great staff support. I have watched and learned as they reviewed expansion opportunities, not just in the United States, but around the world. They are extremely skilled at assessing risks and both are great advisors about community issues. They have developed strong people and find ways to enhance employee opportunities and connect Liberty to great community causes.

The long-term strategy is clear. Resource needs and facility issues are carefully reviewed so that decisions about staffing needs are in line with over-all corporate plans. The company's ledership is, like all the other companies, front and center in the community and takes a turn supporting major regional efforts.

They believe in enhancing the benefits offered to all their employees with terrific training opportunities as well as focusing on customer retention and service. This company also carefully documents and takes the appropriate time to get all the pertinent information about companies they wish to acquire.

Their "due diligence" is just that -- making sure that they have gotten great value for any company purchased or any division sold.

CVS

Tom Ryan of CVS - the wonderful drug store and consumer "goodies" store. I call it "my cosmetics and a whole lot more" store. Tom is ably supported in the personnel area by Mike Ferdinandi, the SVP of Human Resources and Corporate Communications.

From photographic supplies and processing, to prescriptions -- from greeting cards and household supplies as well as a very carefully researched assortment of food, books, snacks and personal care items, CVS provides a handy place to shop. The company wants you to have convenience, parking at or near the front door (even at malls) and products to make your life easier.

Tom has perfected the art of quickly getting information related to issues and confirming a strategy to attack issues or problems. He can focus. His expansion and market plans are great lessons for anyone trying to increase market share and his team focuses on bringing great products at great prices to the consumer. They watch the competition and plan accordingly.

The clipless coupon (a first in America) and the Extra Care Card (which was designed to give shoppers a special discount and a rebate based on their spending total) are marketing marvels, appreciated by those who shop at CVS!

This innovative idea, conceived by Helena Foulkes, the Senior Vice President of Advertising and Marketing, and executed by a tremendous team both internally and exter-nally, has had incredible success. The Extra Care Card is now regarded as THE premiere customer loyalty program in America with over 39,000,000 members!!!

The company makes community participation a priority and constantly reviews its policies and procedures since customer contact and service are viewed as critical. They have also provided specialized training for our employees.

Thank you - and thanks to Sue Murray, Anne Gifford, Jane Van Faasen, Sally Countryman, Debbie Kelly and Cathy Ryan. Thank you for your incredible hospitality. I appreciate your support and for clapping so loudly when you have been in the audience when I have spoken.

What did you note in the descriptions? Negotiating skills, planning, focus, energy, support for staff, community involvement, networking, taking time for family, innovation, creativity, long-term commitments, plans for the future, encouraging others to grow professionally and the list goes on. Take time to review these brief reports and make your own list:

Which leaders do you watch? What have you learned from them?

Do you have mentors?

Who are they?

Have you been a mentor?

I served as a mentor for over six years to a young woman from Boston. We both helped each other. I learned a lot from her and was able to do some things for her that she would not have been able to do on her own. I made a deal with her when I told her that my husband and I would work with her through her high school graduation; right through graduation from college, since this was her dream.

The deal was "NO B'S." I wasn't referring to her grades. I told her that I would applaud her effort if she honestly did her best. I told her that she didn't have to get all A's -- just no B's.

The B's are:
                    ■ No Booze

■ No Boys -- and

■ No Babies

I am proud to report that that young woman, Keisha Gamble graduated from Northeastern University and I was there when they called her name. She is a wonderful young woman and I know that her life will be different because of the time we spent together.

What have you done to encourage someone?

What has that meant to you?

I encourage you to get a mentor for your world of work. You can learn by talking with the mentor about every day issues as well as the big decisions you have to make about your career and your life.

Do you have a mentor at work?

Is there someone you could ask to serve as a mentor?

What do you think you need to focus on with a mentor?

How will you get a mentor?

What are the first steps?

IF YOU WANT A MENTOR
If you are seeking a mentor at your work place, ask someone you admire if they will serve as your mentor. Make sure that if the

person says yes, you have clear ground rules. You should have a plan that covers your contact schedule. Once a month, once a week or something that fits into both of your schedules. Mentors are a great resource so if you feel you can benefit from this help and guidance, design a plan to secure a mentor.

MENTORING A YOUNG ADULT

If you are interested in mentoring a young adult, just check the web address -- mentoring. org. -- for information about this wonderful opportunity. Both you and a child will benefit from your help.

Notes:_____

_____

_____

_____

_____

_____

_____

_____

_____

_____

_____

_____

_____

_____

_____

_____

_____

Chapter 21

NEXT STEPS

Now that we have reviewed some of the tips to help you succeed, to grow and expand; you have to take it from here.

Remind yourself about the skills, talents and gifts that you possess. Challenge yourself to improve them. Find ways to enhance them. Make certain that you explore and learn. In every instance, have a plan. Think ahead.

Be patient, but always look to the future while not forgetting to enjoy the day. Have fun and take time for yourself and your loved ones.

You can reach your goals. You can succeed. It takes will, energy and determination. It takes planning and, the most important thing of all, it takes making the first step.

May you continue to have God's blessings as you travel this great adventure called life!!!

Proverbs 34:10
Those who seek the Lord lack no good thing.

Ecclesiastes 9:10
Whatever your hand does, do it with all your strengths and might.

Ephesians 4:27
Never give place to the devil.

Acts 16:31
Believe on the Lord Jesus Christ and thou shalt be saved, and thy house.

Philippians 4:14
I can do all things through Christ who strengthens me

Philippians 4:6
Be anxious for nothing, but in everything by prayer and
supplication, with thanksgiving, let your requests be made known
to God.

I Thessalonians 5:16, 21, 18
Rejoice always.   Test all things; hold fast what is good.   In
everything give thanks; for this is the will of God in Christ Jesus for
you.

> "To fill the hour - that is happiness.
> Ralph Waldo Emerson

> "Happiness is like a sunbeam, shining on you and those
> around you."
> Anonymous

> "Great things are only possible with outrageous requests."
> Thea Alexander

> "The most difficult thing in the world is to appreciate what
> we have - until we lose it."
> Anonymous

> "The giant oak tree is but an acorn that held its ground."
> Anonymous

> "Speed is good when wisdom has cleared the way."
> Edward R. Murrow

> "Perhaps too much of everything is as bad as too little."
> Edna Ferber

"I don't believe, I know."

Carl Jung

Notes:_____

_____

_____

_____

_____

_____

_____

_____

_____

_____

_____

_____

_____

_____

_____

_____

_____

_____

_____

_____

_____

_____

FINAL NOTES

HAVE A PLAN

ONE STEP AT A TIME

"SPEND TIME WITH THOSE YOU LOVE AND THOSE WHO LOVE YOU."

As you review the messages in this book and the notes you have made, I hope that you have been encouraged and have confirmed your desire to "move to the next level" of leadership. I didn't say it would be easy or that everyone was just going to move aside and clear a path for you. What I have said and what I have experienced is that there are many people who will help you to succeed and want to see you succeed. You need to make certain that you know who they are and seek their guidance and support.

Remember to make time for the important people in your life and take time for yourself. Challenge yourself and, if necessasry, make plans to go back to school. Really focus on what you want to do for the next chapter of your life. Have I had problems? Yes. Have I failed at things? Absolutely. Have I made those mid-course corrections and had to start all over again? I need only tell you about the pages I left on the floor as I typed the many, many drafts for this book and my other book called, "Take Time." These books, however, prove the point of so much of what I have said. A dream come true, with very careful planning, goals and timetables.

Remember, no one can take that first step for you. Good luck as you take that first step in fulfilling your dreams and becoming the leader you want to be.

****

Acknowledgements

(To these great friends - most of whom "danced at our wedding.)

Great Connecticut friends of over 50 years:

> The SSL's and high school friends
> Kathy Clark and Jack
> Carolyn Thorne *
> Joan Gallos
> Kathleen "Corky" Greene
> Nancy Murray
> Eve Smith and Brian
> Jackie and Richie Jankura
> Gail Lupariello
> Judy Curran
> Arlene Brandenberg and Gene
> Evelyn Thayer and Mike
> Annette Cullen and Irv
> Rosemary Lankton and Jack
> Judy A. Solo
> Ann Roviello
> Carolyn Martin
> Frannie Wadeka
> Mary Sandburg and Bruce
> Natalie Siavrakas and Mike
> AND
> Carol Ciraulo from the 5th grade and Joe

AND

Other very special friends of over 40 years:

> Margaret "Pickles" and Bobby MacIntosh
> Rita and Melvin Hayes
> Suzy and Bobby Long
> Marlene and Peter George

Midgie and Chris Tavares
Martha and Kenny Tavares
Hazel and George McNair
Anna and Doris* Mellow
Terri Thompson and Silvino "Val" Valeriano
Beverly Lewis
Jim and Anna Christie
Mary and Earl Mellow

From College

Juliette Bethea

Great Friend and Pen Pal Extraordinaire

Jane Zanardi and her husband, Peter
(We have exchanged weekly letters since 1963)

---

*Deceased

Notes:

A BIG DREAM REALIZED
The Millennium Fund for Children and Families. On April 15, 2003
we held a special reception to celebrate the completion of a
$30,000,000 Fund, almost a year ahead of schedule. To those whose
support and dedication to others has and will continue to make the
greater Boston community a safer and better place
for poor children and their families.
Thank you for making a big dream come true!!!
The formal dedication will be held on September 18, 2003

FleetBoston Financial
Mr. Edmund N. Ansin
Josh and Anita Bekenstein
Mr.* and Mrs. William F. Connell
Martha H. W. Crowninshield
Scott and Laurie Schoen
State Street Corporation
Jeff and Penny Vinik
Darlene and Jerry Jordan
Citizens Financial Group
Liberty Mutual Group
Rod and Lori King Rohda
Jean C. Tempel
James and Jane Wilson
C. Hunter and Pamela T. Boll
CVS Corporation
Paul and Sandy Edgerley
Russell L. Epker and Ann E. Percival
Tim and Corinne Ferguson and family
The Goldberg Family Foundation
Carol, Avram, Deborah and Joshua
   Goldberg, Trustees
Larry and Beth Greenberg
Mr. and Mrs. Robert K. Kraft
Margarete E. and John A. McNeice, Jr.
Tom and Nancy Shepherd
Mr. and Mrs. Norman Silverman
David A. Spina and Stephanie H. Spina
Mr. and Mrs. Peter S. Voss
Mr. Robert L. Beal
Blue Cross Blue Shield of Massachusetts
Ami K. and William A. Danoff
Hilary and Chris Gabrieli

The Harbert Family
Mr. and Mrs. J. Atwood Ives
Jonathan and Jeanne Lavine
Diane and Nick Lopardo
Carolyn and Peter S. Lynch
Cathy E. Minehan and E. Gerald Corrigan
New England Financial
NSTAR
Mark E. Nunnelly and Denise Dupré
Tom and Carol O'Donnell
David R. and Muriel K. Pokross
Ben and Kate Taylor
Bill and Jane Van Faasen
Wellington Management Company, LLP
The Stride Rite Corporation
Ted and Joan Benard-Cutler
Mr. and Mrs. John P. Hamill
Marian and Winlow Heard and Family
Howard and Michele Kessler
Mr. and Mrs. Jonathan O. Lee
Mr. and Mrs. Caleb Loring, Jr.
Tom and Donna May
Ms. Gail McGovern
Marie and Paul O'Brien
Paul F. and Elizabeth A. Quirk
Steve and Robin Scari
Phyllis Yale and Tucker Taft
John R. and Margaret B. Towers
Abrams Family Charitable Trust
Leo and Susan Breitman
Mr. and Mrs. Peter A. Brooke
Kevin and Julie Callaghan
Beth and Linzee Coolidge

Mary and Dan Dennis
Deanna and Tony DiNovi
John R. and Meri P. Grumbacher
Ira and Martha Jackson
Roger and Dawn Kafker
Mr. and Mrs. Edward H. Ladd
Mr. and Mrs. George M. Lovejoy, Jr.
Robert and Kathleen Mahoney
Chester R. and Joyce C. Messer
David and Lauren Murphy
William and Nancy Mutterperl
Mr. Daniel A. and Rev. Diana W.
   Phillips
Charlotte and Irving W. Rabb
Mr. and Mrs. William L. Saltonstall
Peter and Alison Small
Michael D. and Pamela K. Webb
Albert and Carol Wilson
James and Sonja Wolfsberg
Lawrence and Carol Begley
Mr. and Mrs. Robert E. Cowden, III
Gail Deegan and William Huddleston
Mr. and Mrs. Richard C. Garrison
Mr. and Mrs. Ronald A. Homer
Linda and Peter Manning
Richard A. and Helene H. Monaghan
Mr. and Mrs. Paul R. Murphy
Joseph H. Rice and Judith A. Aronstein
Sean C. Rush
Joseph and Deidre Smialowski
Edwin E. and Katharine T. Smith
Ralph and Kathleen Verni
Charlie and Steve Wagner
Michael and Rose* Zoob
Peter F. Carroll
Kathleen M. and Joseph W. Dello Russo
Mr. and Mrs. William E. Duggan
Michael and Barbara Eisenson
Robert J. and Marybeth Haynes
Mr. Thomas O'Neill, III
James W. and Margaret H. Perkins
Kathryn F. Plazak
Helen Chin Schlichte
Mr. and Mrs. Edwin G. Smith
Alan and Lorraine Bressler

Cheryl* and Michael Carson
Meredith and Eugene Clapp
Mr. and Mrs. Anthony T. Cope
Edith Derman
Ernest J. Dieterich
Ray and Kelly Dunn
Andrew and Ana Flaster
Nancy C. and Arthur W. Grellier
Paul S. Grogan and Karen A.
   Sonnarburg
Rev. Raymond Hammond, M.D.
   Rev. Gloria White-Hammond, M.D.
   and the
   Bethal African Methodist Church
Carolyn Golden Hebsgaard
Wilbur T. and Elizabeth M. Hooven
Ted C. Johnson
Guy Lombardo
Mr. and Mrs. John Lowell
Jane and Thomas Martin
Dorick and Priscilla Mauro
Susan Higginson McVeigh
Dr. Elsa Nunez and Dr. Richard
   Freeland
Diane and Deval Patrick
Peter and Suzanne Read
Mrs. Paton R. Roberts
The Estate of Seymour Rothchild
Carl and Fay Simons Family
Micho and Bill Spring
Lenore E. Tagerman
Albert and Judith Zabin
Kathleen A. Casavant
Maria Helena DaSilva
Barbara Jentis
William and Cynthia Marcus
Charlotte B. Read
Sheldon and Roberta Schoen
Juanita and Kenneth Wade
Andrew and Bliss Austin Spooner
Rev. Wesley C. Blount, Jr. and Renee
   Scott Blount
Patricia Brandes
Marilyn Anderson Chase
Joseph and Diane Coughlin

The Curran Family
Charles B. and Leslie E. Gordon
Matthew and Patricia Keenan
Mary Kay Leonard and Richard Valachovic
Colin and Jeanne Maclaurin
Mary Moschos
John A. Ross
Robert Sarason
Meredith L. Singer and Alan J. Chandler *in honor of their wedding*
Kevin and Karen Stone
Rick Tagliaferri and Jill Mackavey
Claudia and Peter Thomas
Andrew and Annemarie Thompson

...also 10 community leaders and two staff members who wish to remain anonymous

* in memoriam

With thanks, appreciation and admiration to:

Mayor Thomas Menino

For his extraordinary leadership and continued support for our combined efforts on behalf of children. His steadfast leadership with United Way's Success by 6 and Keeping Kids on Track initiatives have led to national award-winning efforts.

In addition, he is a partner in the After-School for All Partnership.

Thank you, Tom, for caring so deeply for others.

Thank you also for making the United Way of Massachusetts Bay the only United Way in America with its own park. On April 15, 2003, the Children's Plaza at Christopher Columbus Park, located on the Boston Harbor, was unveiled. This Plaza is dedicated to the children of Boston and all of New England and will allow them to play freely because strangers cared.

To my benefactor,

an individual who has graciously supported the artist in me!!!

Ronald Druker

Thank you. Thank you. Thank you.

This book is also a reminder to say "thank you" - a lot - and lists the key leaders who serve on the United Way Board of Directors. Those leaders are joined by this list of the leaders - the Chairs and Co-Chairs of both our award-winning annual campaigns and those who helped lay the groundwork for the #1 Alexis deTocqueville Society in America. Thank you all!!!

GENERAL CHAIRS - ANNUAL CAMPAIGNS:
John Hamill, Robert Shafto, Joe Faherty, Ron Homer, Helen Chin Schlichte, Joel Alvord, Bill Taylor, Don Reed, Jim DiStasio, Tom May, Chad Gifford, Chet Messer, Ted Kelly, Bob Beal, Bob and Myra Kraft and Bob and Kathleen Mahoney.

CHAIR - CO-CHAIRS, de TOCQUEVILLE SOCIETY:
Carol Goldberg, Peter Lynch, Bill Taylor, Tom O'Donnell, Russ Epker, Martha Crowninshield, Mitch Kertzman, Paul O'Brien, Sandy Edgerely, Bob Beal and Jim DiStasio.

We are appreciative of your help and, most important of all, what these funds have allowed us to do to support children and needy families.

For the Religious leaders in my life:

      *Rev. William O. Johnson, long-term Pastor of the First Baptist Church in Stratford, Connecticut

      Rev. Dr. and Mrs.Michael Ellis of Columbus Avenue AME Zion Church in Boston, Massachusetts.

      Evangelist Dorothy Allsop, long time family friend of Bridgeport,Connecticut

      Rev. George Sanders, Presiding elder and former pastor of the Walter's Memorial AME Zion Church,, Bridgeport, Connecticut

      Rev. and Mrs. Timothy Howard, Pastor, Walter's Memorial AME Zion Church in Bridgeport, Connecticut

      Father Charles Allen, former President, Fairfield College Preparatory School, Fairfield, Connecticut

      Father Aloyisious Kelly, President, Fairfield University, Fairfield, Connecticut

---

*Deceased

Leaders who have supported us "early on" and continue to help in personal and special ways like hosting the Heards and, also, checking on us from time to time:

We appreciate the quiet dinners and your very special support. It means a lot to both of us.

Paul and Marie O'Brien
Tom and Carol O'Connell
Mike Carson and Ed Ansin
Michele Courton Brown and Philip Brown
Frances and Bud Moseley
Liz and Ed Dugger
Josephine McNeil
Jim and Cathy Stone
Milton and Jimmy Hagins
Verniece and Isaiah Owen
John and Margarete McNiece
Howard and Michele Kessler
Nancy Korman
Carol Bolling Fulp
Jerry Martinson
Sheryl Marshall
Frank and Jamie McCourt
Kevin and Ann Phelan
Dick Glovsky
Nick and Diane Lopardo
Lois and Norm Silverman
And former Bostonians
Ira and Martha Jackson

FOR ADDITIONAL INFORMATION CONTACT:

MARIAN L. HEARD
CHAIRMAN AND CEO
HEARD ENTERPRISES, LLC
P.O. BOX 811
NATICK, MASS. 01760
e-mail: wmheard@aol.com

Quantity discounts available
for 10 or more copies.

Notes: